"As I looked through *Program ~~~~~~~*, my life passed before my eyes. This book is a priceless gift to the eager, hard-working, new speech and drama teacher...stressing the positive...admitting the frustrations...knowing that everyone who has chosen this path experiences the same exhilarations and despairs."

> Annette Lewis, Speech & Drama Teacher

"What a magnificent 'advice book', a must for beginning speech and drama teachers. I am so pleased with this sharing of thirty years of successful experience. *Program Building* has a very wise, common sense attitude toward teaching, walking the line between the demands of students and administrators."

> Dr. Thomas McDonald, Curriculum Director
> Phoenix Union High School District

"This book would be an excellent complement to the material presented in my courses, providing young teachers with solid, helpful advice on the management of a total program."

> Karen Kay Husted, Adjunct Professor of
> Education, University of Phoenix

"*Program Building* should be on the resource shelf of any school administrator who supervises student activities, interscholastic coaches, campus facilities, or program directors, and in the resource library of English & Performing Arts Departments."

> Martha T. Davis, Ed. D.
> Supervisor of English & Performing Arts
> Phoenix Union High School District (Retired)

PROGRAM BUILDING

A Practical Guide for High School Speech and Drama Teachers

Toby Heathcotte

Mardel Books

Mardel Books
6145 West Echo Lane
Glendale, AZ 85302

©2003 by Toby Heathcotte

ISBN 0-9640882-6-6

Library of Congress Control Number 2002094546

Program Building: A Practical Guide for High School Speech and Drama Teachers is a revision of *Stuff I Wish I'd Known: A Practical Guide for High School Speech and Drama Teachers*, first released as a trade paperback in 1994 and updated as an Ebook in 2000.

Some images @ 2003 www.clipart.com.

Dedication

For the brave and creative men and women who teach speech and drama in the high schools of the twenty-first century.

Acknowledgments

Thanks go to the following people for their presence in my life:

- my longtime friends and school chums, Jacque Beatty, Nancy Brehm, Betty Joy, and Maggie Perry, for helping me to believe in myself and my ability to write;
- my sons, Brandy and Brock, for their love and willingness over the years to debrief me at the end of a day's teaching;
- the staff of the Carl Hayden Computer Magnet for technical support;
- my niece Tearle Dwiggins for inspiring this book;
- and especially about four thousand former students for their bright entrances and loving exits across the stage of my teaching career.

Preface

This book is not about content. I assume you learned your content in college. It's not about lesson planning either. If you got your teaching license, you've already had classes in how to plan and execute a lesson. This book is a practical guide to the process of being a speech and drama teacher. How to do it, day by day, and survive in today's high school—that's the subject of this book…stuff I wish I'd known when I started out.

I've been a high school speech and drama teacher for thirty years and a performing arts department chair for ten of those years. I helped design the auditorium and classroom wing for Carl Hayden High School in Phoenix and ran the auditorium for fifteen years. I've coached drama all of that time. I started the first speech team at my school and have been the coach for twenty years. I've served on the Arizona Interscholastic Association Speech and Theatre Advisory Board and as an officer of the Forensic League of Arizona. I've hosted many tournaments, including State Finals twice. I've taught between three thousand and four thousand students over those years.

In my thirtieth year of teaching I became both more selfish and more altruistic at the same time. By taking early retirement, I found another career as a college instructor and a writer, something I've always wanted. I have always loved being a speech and drama teacher, and my career successes have come in that area, probably for that reason.

On leaving high school teaching, I hoped for some continuity with new teachers coming in. I want to share what I've learned and tell what's worked for me for the good of the order. That's the reason for this book.

If I share with you what I have learned, at the end of your thirty years or whenever you leave, you will have contributed much to the art of teaching speech and drama. I will have been a part of your experience. My influence, my ideas, my love for the work go on forever…and so do yours.

Toby Heathcotte
Glendale, Arizona

Foreword

Now that you have finished teacher training, you are ready to be an effective educator. You know how to do lesson plans and how to out-psych the students before they out-psych you, theoretically. But do you know how to avoid buying something during every fund-raiser, something which will either make you fat or be resold at a yard sale? Do you know how to avoid living to work, rather than working to live? You will find that kind of information in this book. And are you ready for the co-curricular assignments, those listed on the job description as "other duties as assigned," which are as much a part of a drama and speech teacher's job as the classroom duties? My guess is that you are not...not until you have read this book. It will help you encounter the positive aspects of being a speech and drama teacher and avoid the negative.

Because I am a veteran speech and drama teacher myself, I thought this book might hold my interest only for a few minutes. As I turned one page after the next, I found myself chuckling, nodding my head, and anxious to read what advice awaited on the next page. I read half of the book in one sitting.

All of what I read is true, not just for the author, but for me, and for many, many other speech and drama teachers whom I have known over the years. When I put the book down, my first thought was, "I wish I had known that stuff!"

Although you may have recently hummed the melody of <u>Pomp and Circumstance</u> as you played follow-the-leader in cap and gown, do not commence to teach your first class until you have finished this book.

Read it. Believe it. There will be a test on it every year of your professional life.

Larry Whitesell
Performing Arts Curriculum Coordinator
Paradise Valley Unified School District
Paradise Valley, Arizona

Table Of Contents

PREFACE

FOREWORD

CHAPTER 1

Handling the Day-to-Day

Much of the impetus for this book grew out of conversations I had with my niece, Tearle Dwiggins, during her first year of teaching. Though she taught computers and accounting in Indiana and I taught speech and drama in Arizona, our concerns were very similar. At my suggestion, she prepared the following list based on this idea:

My first year as a teacher would have been easier if only I'd known....

—how to benefit from the opening-of-school meetings

You'll probably be hit by a barrage of acronyms that every one else seems to know the meaning for. They vary from school to school and so can't be categorized, but they'll probably sound something like SIT/COR, RENAISSANCE, CTA, CEA, DSO, CES, etc. It's important to learn the meanings, but you could possibly teach twenty years in a school and not know them all, so relax.

Look before you sit in faculty meetings. Find two or three teachers who are forty-plus years old, sitting together, talking, and obviously glad to see each other after summer vacation. These teachers are the backbone of the campus and are willing and happy to answer your questions, like "What does SIT/COR stand for?"

—what to do with the kids on the first day of school

Show them the books you're going to use during the course; explain any requirements, such as keeping a journal, bringing a pen, being on time...management stuff. Explain school policies, such as the bell schedule, attendance monitoring, and gun laws

Play the name game or some other ice breaker, so you can get to know the kids and they can get to know you. The name game is this: The student in the first chair says his or her own name; the second student says the first student's name, then his or her name; the third student says the first student's name, the second student's name, then his or her own name; and so on around the room until the last person must say the names of everyone in the room.

If the bell hasn't rung yet, make a brainstorming list on the board of things we like to know about new people in our lives, like hobbies, interests, musical preferences, number of brothers and sisters. Then, divide the students into pairs and ask them to interview each other to find out the things on the list. After a few minutes, ask each set of pairs to stand and introduce their partner to the class. If the bell hasn't rung by now, punt.

—how to avoid feeling isolated from other teachers

Boredom quotient—the bigger the school district, the longer and dryer the opening of school convocation. However, you can't beat it for people watching, and teachers are some of the most interesting people to watch...probably because they're used to sixty-six eyes per period fixed unswervingly on their every movement, especially the one that turns their back to the class for an instant. Seriously, watching teachers relate to each other warms the heart because they genuinely love each other, and they're full of vitality at the opening of school meetings, wanting to share with each other.

To watch them do that and to introduce yourself as you get an opportunity can be rewarding. Don't be shy. Just walk up to a friendly looking group of teachers, and say "Hi, I'm _____(insert your own name here), and I'm going to be teaching speech and drama at Walt Whitman High this year." That's all you'll have to say because the other teachers will take over from there, ask you more questions than you probably want to answer, and introduce you to more people than you really want to know.

—what to do with the kids the day before vacation

Plan something more upbeat and fun than the usual school day. Stretch it a little if you have to, but keep them interested. Get into the holiday spirit. For example, turn out the lights the day before Halloween; then have the students sit in a circle and tell ghost stories to each other.

One of the first vacation holidays will be Thanksgiving. Unless you're a history teacher, don't do the Puritan/Indian thing. The kids will be antsy, so plan an activity that gets them up and moving. You could do an improvisation or impromptu speeches based on "my best or worst Thanksgiving" or "what I'd be doing if I were ditching school today."

Such an assignment could establish a kind of tradition in your class. If you're a bit clever and creative, the kids will look forward to coming to your class on the day before vacation. Then, you can sneak in some educational gamesmanship, like assigning research for Christmas stories from different cultures a week in advance. Then the day before vacation, the class can sit around with cupcakes in hand and tell each other Christmas stories from lands far away.

--the fairest grading system, that's also easy for the teacher

A grading system based on points is probably the fairest one from the point of view of students. People see letters, such as A, B, C, as subjective; but they see numbers as objective. Actually, all grading is subjective in the sense that it is a judgment of performance. When you assign an informative speech or a pantomime and give it a 50-point value, you will split numbers in substantially the same way you would award a letter grade. For example, an A performance will get 46 to 48 points, a B performance 40, and so on.

It's important for you to understand the subjectivity of all performance work. A student's grade is always your judgment of the quality of his or her performance. That's just the way it is. Given this knowledge, a numbered grading system will probably cut down on a lot of the complaints you receive when report cards come out. Just consult your grade book, add the numbers again, and tell the student what he or she has earned. Seeing the numbers in black and white will usually satisfy the student.

You can make the point system easy to work with by giving values in multiples of 5 or 10, whatever is easy for you. I know a teacher who gives high point values, like 250 points for a one-page paper. Then, at the end of the grading period, the teacher spends a lot of time with a calculator for no good reason. Oh, I know there are computer software programs that make all these calculations for you. I also know you have to input all those numbers first. It's just as easy and efficient to give a smaller point value. Here is a sample from one grading period in a speech class. It's easily adaptable to any other subject area.

10 points – introduction of partner
10 points - fear speech
15 points - questions at the end of Chapter 2
10 points - outline for process speech
50 points - process speech
10 points - impromptus on winning a lottery
25 points - critique of a process speech
15 points - debate vocabulary
15 points - questions at the end of Chapter 7
20 points - outline for debate with partner

20 points - 10 case cards for first debate

50 points - first debate

This sample sets up a 250-point scale for a 9-week grading period. You can convert it to a 60-percent level of competency like this:

60 percent of 250 is 150, the baseline passing grade.

250 less 150 is 100. Divided by 4 grades of A, B, C, and D (or 1, 2, 3, and 4), you get 25 points for each grade division. That translates to:

225 to 250 = A or 1

200 to 224 = B or 2

175 to 199 = C or 3

150 to 174 = D or 4

If you have a problem with attendance or tardies at your school (and who doesn't?), you might want to consider giving points for being there and also for being there on time. You can give 2 points for being present but only 1 if the student was late. That's fairly easy to calculate at the end of the grading period. If there are 45 days in a grading period, add 90 to your total of points for grades. Then count up the absences and tardies, subtracting 2 points for each absence and 1 point for each tardy.

Your first year of teaching you'll probably want to just use your own assignments for calculating your grade. However, giving point values for attendance can help, particularly if your school administration is somewhat lax in that area. If your administration assesses major consequences for absences or tardies, then you can ignore this component of the grade.

—what work to take a grade on and what to simply check

If you expect the students to write an assignment to turn in or if you expect them to prepare for an oral performance, give them points for their effort. I personally never check anything in the grade book without giving it a point value; I either give it points or don't ask for it to be turned in. I always give points when a student performs before the class, even in an impromptu or improvisational situation. Effort should always receive a reward in the classroom.

—how to decide how much each assignment, activity, and test should be worth

Before you assign a point value, think about what you want the students to accomplish. Do you want them to understand something and then show you that they understand? Then give them a few points for demonstrating understanding, 10 or 15 points for vocabulary or answering questions.

Do you want the students to create something, requiring a real effort on their part, such as a speech or a duo acting scene? If so, make the points commensurate with the assignment.

In summary, the point value for each assignment should reflect the amount of effort required to accomplish it.

—an objective way to give a reward for effort

Bonus points are an excellent way to reward students. You can give them for effort. Or, you can give them for extra work. Or, you can give them for helping you grade papers. Or, you can give them for running the sound system at an assembly. Or, you can give them for really anything you want to give them for. Bonus means above and beyond the requirements of a course. If a student does work at this level, give him or her points that will reflect in a better grade.

Another good way to reward effort is to write a note home to the parents and simply say, "Sally is turning in her homework every day, and she always has a smile for me and the other students." Now, what parent would not like such a note to come home? What student would not get a positive charge out of that kind of a connection between the parent and the teacher?

Don't be afraid to communicate with the home. The more positive the interaction with the home, the better it is for the student, the parent, and the teacher. If you can think of something good to say about your students, say it. You can even put yourself on a schedule, something like this: write a letter home for at least one student in every class every week. That's lots of good vibes for everyone

—a system for keeping track of makeup work so it doesn't pile up until the end of the grading period

Makeup work is a tricky business. It's like the regular work in the class; and, at the same time, it isn't. For your own peace of mind, try to conform the makeup work to the regular class work as much as possible. That's particularly difficult in performance work because there's nothing that can really replace giving a speech before a class. If a student is out sick, you're probably better off giving reading and writing assignments, even ones that involve research; but, hold off on oral assignments until the student actually returns to school.

Another part of this subject has to do with the teacher's self-discipline. It's critically important to stay on top of your own paperwork, whether student assignments or mail. Form the habit of setting aside a certain period of time that is inviolate, such as the first half hour after you arrive on campus in the morning or the last before you leave. You might have a preparation period that allows you privacy. Whenever it is, make sure you have such a time to keep current on your own paperwork.

During that time, read your mail, process it as seems necessary, and keep your grade book up to date with entries for current assignments and makeup work. Don't fall behind in this detail, even if you have to stay a little late to keep current. Otherwise, you could be setting yourself up for a stressful episode. Then, you'll have to deal with stress, a depressingly time-consuming activity.

—*how to balance time between school and home*

Time at school and time away from school have a way of blending together, and your life can come apart at deadline time for grades or the night of a performance. Keep a time management or day book visible on your desk. Include your school commitments, such as performances and meetings, dentist appointments, doing laundry, dates or other social activities, your mother's birthday, and anything else that requires a share of your time.

If you notice that you're out of coffee in the morning, write "get coffee" in your day book. Don't even expect to remember to stop at the grocery on the way home from school. Your mind will be full of fixing a scene that doesn't work or worrying about some student who has mysteriously stopped coming to school. Next thing you know it's morning and there's no coffee. That's a pretty grumpy way to start a day.

—how to prioritize school responsibilities

Sometimes teachers get stressed because they think every single thing they do is equally important; that is, faculty meetings, parent/teacher conferences, grading papers, planning for classes. It all becomes a swirl of obligations. The question is which to do first, how long, and what to skimp on, if necessary.

There is no right or wrong answer to this quandary. A rule of thumb is: The greater the impact on the student, the higher the priority. Therefore, teaching the kids in front of you is more important than grading papers; planning for your classes is more important than a faculty meeting; a parent conference is more important than lunch in the cafeteria.

Keeping a balance is the best policy. If you continually miss faculty meetings to grade papers, you could put your job in jeopardy. Just use your common sense and relax a little.

—how to deal with a classroom of students who bring out the worst in each other

Sometimes a student misbehaves in every teacher's class. Administrators usually know this kind of student well. Simply asking the administrator in charge of discipline what he or she knows about the student will give you a hint as to whether you've got this kind of student. If so, tell the student in very clear words what you expect in his or her behavior. If you don't get that behavior, write a referral or otherwise follow your school's discipline procedures.

One note on writing referrals: Be clear and specific about the objectionable behavior, even if that means quoting a swear word on the referral. Don't say, "Johnny misbehaves in class or Johnny shows disrespect." Say instead, "Johnny threw the pencil sharpener on the floor and jumped on it nine times, yelling 'Yahoo' loudly."

Wait a reasonable length of time, like a day or two, before you follow up on a referral. After all, administrators are busy, too. However, if you've not heard anything on the third day, ask what happened. You want to know whether or not Johnny is headed for the gas chamber.

The more common kind of discipline problem is the kind referred to in this section title...where kids key on each other. Often times when a group of students misbehave day after day, you've got one or two students who are leading them into that behavior.

Notice how your students interact when they are misbehaving. At whom do they look? To whom do they address questions? To whom do they listen? The answers you get will tell you who the leaders are.

Once you've figured out who is really causing the problem, talk to the student(s), one at a time. Tell them that you are having trouble getting the class to cooperate. Tell them you need the cooperation of the whole group in order to do your job. Tell them that, without cooperation, very little learning can take place; and it's your job to see that the learning does take place. Tell them that you have noticed their leadership ability and their popularity. Ask them to help you lead the class in a more positive direction. Ask them if they will help you keep order in the class.

If that doesn't work...and you'll know in one or two days...then try moving students around in the classroom. When you do that, tell them the reason you are moving students is so that you can get more cooperation and a better learning environment.

It's always good to be honest with kids. If you don't tell them what you're doing, they'll know anyway. Whatever you do, don't lie to them by making up some other reason for moving their seats. If you lie to them, they'll lose respect for you...not good for you or them.

—how not to take personally students' poor behavior

Have a wide view. There are many different reasons why students misbehave. Here's a sample list:
     —mad at girl friend or boyfriend

—mad at parent

—mad at brother or sister

—mad at another teacher

—mad at some other school employee

—mad at a friend

—mad at a smart aleck in another class

—mad at the world

—mad at themselves

—mad at you

Those odds aren't too shabby. Now, let's say that it's the one in ten shot, and a student is seriously mad at you. Either it's justified or it's not. If it's justified, apologize to the student. If it's not justified, then blow it off. You're not responsible for your students' emotions.

—*that a fair portion of a teacher's salary goes to purchasing items sold by students*

Students will try with earnest eyes and eager smiles to sell you candy, Christmas cards, marathon miles, key chains, carwashes, etc., etc., etc. The students who try to sell them to you are usually the most conscientious and dear students you have. They are the very students it's most difficult to say no to.

My advice is to say yes. Just buy one of whatever sale is going around; then tell the other students who ask that you bought from "Joe." They'll be mildly annoyed because you didn't buy from them, but they'll be glad you bought from someone.

Some additional pointers: always buy from the first person who asks you, so students won't feel that you're playing favorites. If you buy more than one item, buy from more than one student. Try to pay in cash so that students won't see your home address and phone number on your check. That could save you some awkward phone calls or unwanted visits later.

Consider the students' sales as your charity, and don't give to the United Way. I recognize that I'll not sell many of these books to people from the United Way, but that's "show biz."

—how not to catch every illness carried by students

Follow Grandma's formula: drink lots of water; eat soup during the flu season; exercise and get lots of sleep; take mega-doses of vitamin C during the winter...do whatever helps you get through the time or the illness.

Also know that, by beginning to be the teacher instead of the student, you have upset a powerful pattern that has worked since you were five or six years old. You are now the teacher, the person in charge of structuring school, instead of the student, passively accepting the structure of others. You are thereby adding a great deal of stress to your life. Stress inhibits the immune system and contributes to making people sick.

There is hope, however. People get sick less often as they learn to cope better with stress in their lives. In the meantime, some people have to really make themselves sick so they won't feel guilty taking a day off now and then for a treat. Don't be one of those people. Help yourself cope by giving yourself rest and relaxation days.

The relationship between attitude and illness is very delicate. I refer you to the work of the Institute of Noetic Sciences for an in-depth study of the subject. But one idea I would like to share: teachers are notorious for getting sick, having surgeries, even dying during Christmas and summer vacations. I think that's because every cell of their bodies believes it is essential to finish school.

—that students don't love school as much as you do

Probably true. But, let's be fair. You probably don't love car repair as much as some of your students do. Or, football. Or, math. You can't believe that everyone doesn't think speech and drama are as important as you do. You love these subjects and have a long time interest in them, but most students don't. The important thing is to do the best you can at teaching your students...then let it go emotionally. Honor yourself for doing a tough job the best you can. Your power has got to come from within.

There's one little side benefit that you will discover as time goes by. Remember that Johnny who caused you so much grief in class and was in and out of the principal's office? Well, he's the same Johnny who's going to grow up and realize how much you cared about him and how much you taught him. And, one day you're going to run into him at the checkout counter at the grocery store; and he's going to thank you for turning his life around. Trust me....it happens. Not every student is as affected by your class, but you can never tell which one will be.

And, here's a twist...you may or may not remember who
he was. But that's okay. You did your job, and Johnny
recognizes that you did and is grateful, whether you ever
run into him at

—how to not worry about a RIF notice

Though I'm sorry to say it's true, RIF (reduction in force)
notices have been a part of teaching for the past several
years. Since the number of teachers depends enormously
on the number of students and since temperamental state
legislatures dictate money amounts allocated to schools, I
expect that RIF notices will be with us for a while.

There's no way to eliminate worry in the situation
where anyone might lose his or her job. I do, however,
have some thoughts about easing concern.

Find out your worst-case scenario as early as possible. Is that being completely unemployed or possibly
going to half time? If you go to half-time, will you keep
your benefits or lose them? Are you in line to get
bumped by teachers from other schools in the district or
not?

Whatever the political realities are in your school
district, know them. Know what's going on with fund-
ing and enrollment ahead of time. Become politically ac-
tive, if necessary.

Loss of enrollment in one school district often
means gains in enrollment in other districts. If you're
teaching in the inner city and you see lots of RIF's, start
looking for a job in the suburbs, or vice versa. Don't wait
until you receive your RIF letter to start looking.

Don't tie yourself to a mortgage or other heavy-duty payments until you feel fairly certain your job is secure.

Remember: you were looking for a job when you found this one; you can look again.

Find a significant other who is not a teacher. No, really....I'm just kidding on this part. It is important to remember, though, that to choose teaching as a career is not without risk. The pay is low; teachers get RIFed; trends in education can ace teachers out of their jobs (look at the rise and fall of physical education, home economics, and dance, to name a few).

Maybe you've chosen teaching as a career for the learning it can bring you. Maybe you'll learn to live with uncertainty...to enjoy the momentary high when a kid really learns something....to know the value of what you do in the moment as a teacher. What else is there, really?

CHAPTER 2

Creating Relationships

Scenario: It's the last play of the year. Just when you think you've got every possible problem solved, the air conditioning goes out in the whole building on the night of your final performance. A sweating audience is getting uglier by the minute. You're sure you'll have to start re-funding tickets. Miraculously, the custodians work over-time to get the air conditioning going again so your show can go up. You smile the biggest "thanks" you've every felt, and the curtain opens.

Creating good working relationships with the other people in your school community can literally make the difference between your success or failure in your job. Certainly an aspect of those relationships, dependent upon the personalities of others and your own personality, is outside the scope of this book. However, another aspect of those relationships is the mutual interdependency that school people share. It is in the spirit of enhancing that mutual interdependency that I offer the ideas below.

—*personal guidelines*

To develop these relationships with others in the school, there are two personal guidelines that I feel are critical to your success. The first is the way you perceive yourself, and the second is the outcome you expect.

See yourself as a program director. Indeed, you are that. Even though your job description may say "teacher,' you have actually been hired to build a program in speech, in drama, or in both. If you see yourself as "just a teacher," you're headed for failure because others will see you that way, also. However, if you see yourself as...capitalized...Director of the Forensics Program or Theatre Director, you will be seen as a person doing important work....building a program, impacting kids, looking to the future. You are all of those things, so you may as well have the respect those titles bring from the very beginning, rather than having to work for it later.

Build win/win relationships. You'll be cultivating relationships with other people in part because you need them to accomplish your goals. Make sure the other people always get what they need out of the liaison, too. Put some extra effort into seeing that others get what gives them a win. It's easy to build a win/win result into a school relationship. When you ask others to do something, also ask them how you can help them or what would make their part of the job go easier; then provide what the others need. As a result, you will find your own wins growing daily.

—*custodians*

One thinks of custodians as people who wash windows, change light bulbs, and empty trash. That's all true, but they do much more. They create the feeling tone of the campus. If the rooms are sparkling and the grounds are well groomed each morning, a cheerful mood is set for the entire campus. It says something like, "You're important. This place is well kept for your benefit." If, on the other hand, the chairs are pushed back carelessly in the rooms, windows are left unclean, and waste baskets are not emptied, a quite different mood prevails, a hostile, cold, and depressing one.

—*custodians and speech teachers*

Over and above their importance to the entire campus, custodians have a special importance to speech teachers. Custodians are often in charge of maintaining the school's vans. Because you often transport students in the vans, you will have a stake in their care and maintenance.

Often you will find that, even though custodians make an effort to maintain the vans, things go wrong while you're at tournament...a battery might die, a tire might go flat, or any of an assortment of things that we all know can go wrong with a motor vehicle. **Always be sure you're carrying a school credit card to pay for these problems on the road.**

When you return to school, talk personally to the custodians, making certain they understand what went wrong with the vehicle and what you've already done to correct the problem.   Be sensitive to the fact that they might be a little embarrassed by your road problems, and let them know that you know it can happen to anyone. Then, next time, you'll probably get a van that's been thoroughly checked out in advance.

In the event that van maintenance becomes a problem and you feel that the safety of students is at risk, don't try to handle the situation yourself. Talk to the assistant principal in charge of vans or in charge of custodians. Make it clear that your concern is to insure the safety of your students and not to criticize the work of another adult on your campus. The last thing in the world you want to do is alienate the individual custodian by creating a situation where his or her job is in jeopardy. On the other hand, your priority has to be the safety of your students while you're out on the road.

—custodians and drama teachers

Drama teachers are even more dependent on custodians for the smooth functioning of their jobs than are speech teachers. Cleaning and maintaining the auditorium are basic to conducting any theatre program. Therefore, it's imperative that drama teachers create good working relationships with their custodians. The two primary ones are the custodian who cleans the auditorium and the head of maintenance for the whole school.

Get to know the custodian who cleans your building on a personal level...not just his or her name, but something about the individual. When your schedules cross, generally at the end of the school day and/or during rehearsal, chat with your custodian. If you feel comfortable inquiring about a spouse or children, do so. If not, simply establish a friendly, work-related relationship. Then, you can feel more confident directing some of the work the custodian does, because it often is essential for you to do so.

Certainly you are the person most directly affected by the work the custodian does. The chances are good that the custodian is aware of this fact, also, and wants to please you. A hint: **Ask** to have light bulbs changed or furniture moved...don't demand. Try also to project your needs a few days ahead, so that you're not always operating out of panic. For example, if you feel it is critical that the stage floor be painted before your show opens, give the custodian some lead time...at least a week in advance, so that he or she can organize the workload.

Bottom line...be kind. "Good afternoon" and "Have a good weekend" said on a regular basis will create much good will and an amiable relationship with a person who is not only in a position to help or hurt your teaching but is also probably a person who takes pride in his or her work and wants things to go well for you.

The head of maintenance at your school is also a very important person to you. The same rules apply to relations with him or her as to your relationship with your building custodian...with one important exception. You would do well to see this person as your equal and co-worker in all respects. You have students to direct and a building to steward. The head of maintenance has a crew of custodians and many buildings to steward.

The two of you have common concerns. Don't get caught in some intellectual trap that says your needs have more value because you have a bachelor's or a master's degree. As sorry as I am to have to admit it, occasionally some teachers do get into that state of mind. If you as a drama teacher get there, you're in trouble, because so many of the people you need to help you do your job adequately don't have degrees. But they do have hearts and minds and needs. Just like you and your students do.

—secretaries, clerks, security guards

There's no magic to creating these relationships. Just as with custodians, appreciation is the key. If they know that you genuinely appreciate them and respect their contribution to the school, they will respond positively to you. Then, you'll be much more able to conduct the business of your job. You'll also be operating from the reality of school life. A school can become pitifully dysfunctional when the school principal's secretary has been out sick for a week. It's quite easy to see the value of support personnel in that circumstance.

What specific tasks these people do and how closely they are related to your job will vary in different schools and at different times in the same school. Activities secretaries are often very important to speech and drama teachers because they schedule vans, take care of student permissions and eligibilities, schedule events in the auditorium, and handle countless other details of your school life.

It's always worth a few moments to get to know these people and establish a personal working relationship. If you want to be a successful teacher, you will make it a practice always to do so. A little side benefit might be that you will find yourself becoming a popular teacher...not too bad for your psyche, either.

—administrators

Administrators come in many varieties, with assorted goals for their jobs. Your relationships with all of them will be partially dependent on their particular jobs, be that student discipline or attendance, facilities, program directors, etc. As a speech or drama teacher, you will often find yourself dealing with the administrators on your campus as well as district-wide administrators in charge of specific programs, such as performing arts, special projects, or competitive events.

Remember that you are a program director when you interact with administrators. Be honest and straightforward about your program needs, such as money, time, facilities, or whatever. You are not "just another teacher." You have responsibility to run your program, and you will be able to do so better if administrators see you in that role.

Be an advocate for your program with your administrators. Invite them to your performances. Show them programs and fliers. Remind them of budgetary needs. Keep them informed about all aspects of your program.

Blow your own horn: let them know how many people were in your audiences, how many of your students received awards or scholarships, how many of your competitors ranked in tournament.

Keep your program in their minds, and make them proud of the job you are doing. If they can go to other schools or the district office and brag about your program, they will be a lot more likely to support you in

your needs. There is no way to beat win/win relationships, so work to create them with your administrators.

There may be times when you will find yourself in the position of having to fight for a particular aspect of your program, like getting some authority over all-school assembly procedures, for example. The more groundwork you have laid in workable, win/win relationships with your administrators, the more success you will have in all aspects of school life.

—*other teachers*

Ralph Waldo Emerson in his essay "Friendship" says this: "A friend is a person with whom I may be sincere. Before him I may think aloud."

For me, relationships with other teachers have been some of the most meaningful components of my teaching career. Other teachers have been my best friends, my mentors, my confidants, and my allies. There is a common bond among teachers that assures fertile territory for friendships. That bond is a blessing of the occupation of teaching.

Teaching is a difficult job. It's demanding, time and energy consuming. All of us need someone to talk to from time to time about these stresses. Other teachers are the most understanding and sympathetic friends you will ever have to fill this need. And the reverse is also true. You can be a good friend to other teachers.

In no part of teaching is this more true than in our area. Because of the nature of our jobs, isolation is often a problem. Drama teachers, especially, are often physically isolated by being housed in the auditorium and not in a regular school building. Because of the need to practice for speech events and rehearse shows, we're often the first car in the parking lot in the morning and the last car out at night. In between we spend practically all of our time with students, even coaching while eating a sack lunch. Therefore, we become isolated from contacts with other teachers. Additionally, we are often the only teacher in our area on the faculty or, at best, one of a few teachers; and, unfortunately, teachers in other subject areas cannot always relate to our teaching problems and needs.

It's important to **build solidarity with other speech and drama teachers** in your school district or in your geographic area. Some of your closest relationships will be forged with them. In my career, these other speech and drama teachers have become lifetime friends.

Not every teacher will be your best friend, of course. In fact some faculties develop factions, sub-groups that side with each other on issues and support each other. Sometimes they go so far as to dislike and/or avoid other subgroups, based on these liaisons.

While you are a new teacher on the faculty, cau-tion might be your best stance here. Certainly it's good to begin establishing collegial relationships with other per-forming arts faculty and with the art and language facul-ties, since there is a built-in kinship with them. But, be-fore joining a subgroup, you might do well to take time to observe and know the political territory on your campus. Then, you can make a more intelligent judgment about any personal or political liaisons you might wish to enter.

There are other relationships with teachers—as colleagues. Some of your best allies and most loyal audi-ence members will come from the English, arts, and lan-guage faculties. I suggest some effort to cultivate these relationships for the win/win's inherent in them. For ex-ample, speech and drama classes often need small audi-ences for in-class performances, perhaps for a readers theatre or improvisational theatre. Make it a practice to invite English teachers and their classes to such events.

You can use these small events for audience build-ing among the student body, for teaching audience behav-ior, and for creating theatrical experiences. Your goals may be informal or formal, even organized and planned in advance with the English teachers. Perhaps you will give a short talk at the beginning of the show about audience behavior (good for freshmen classes) or explain readers theatre to more advanced classes.

For main stage productions, make sure every teacher gets a complementary ticket. Whether they use it or not, there is pleasure in receiving the free ticket and some easy advertising for your production. You also might see some teachers turn up and pay their significant other's way in.

Such activities build good will among the faculty. Then, perhaps, you won't get so many complaints from teachers if you take their students out of class for tournaments, performances, or technical work at assemblies.

These activities also help in the advocacy of your program, an ongoing part of your role as speech and/or drama teacher.

—*students*

Relationships with students are exceedingly important for you. I personally have found that there is no generality about relationships with students. They are instead specific to the personalities of the students and to the framework in which you get to know them. Therefore, I refer you to these chapters where I discuss relationships with students, specific to Starting a Speech Team, Directing the First Show, and Running an Auditorium.

—*parents*

Because of your after-school-hours relationships with your students, you're going to get to know their parents better than a regular teacher does. Sometimes that can be negative, for example when a parent decides to pull the student out of a show or tournament for disciplinary reasons or simply out of selfishness, like needing the student to baby-sit.

It's times like that you'll probably be tempted to kill the parent or at least give him or her a piece of your mind. I suggest the latter, done tactfully. If other students and you are depending on the student to perform a role, that thought should be communicated. Students need to learn at school that they are responsible for fulfilling the commitments they voluntarily make. You need to tell the parents you are trying to instill that trait in your students.

It may feel sometimes that you are teaching the parent about responsibility and commitment, and the truth is that you may be. So...do it. You're a teacher, aren't you? It's important to remember that you won't always win in these situations, but that's okay. You need to try. Often, the student will be very happy if you do

On the other hand, lots of relationships with parents are excellent. You will probably find yourself becoming friendly with them because you share a common interest...their child. In fact, it's possible that you can increase positive relationships with parents by creating a parent organization to support your speech and/or drama activities.

An obvious benefit is that parents get to be a part of their children's activities at school. They can perform very meaningful services, too, such as raising money for out-of-town speech trips or sewing costumes for a musical. Even something so simple as having parents provide refreshments at intermission of a play helps to create a feeling of belonging and being "in it" together.

Your students can brainstorm ways to involve parents in your program. Some probably have businesses or talents, which will work into your program. For example, a parent who works in a T-shirt shop might make T-shirts for your speech team. A parent who is a minister might talk about stage fright or speech preparation. A parent who is retired military might coach your actors on walking and talking like a soldier.

The ways to involve parents in your program are endless. It is worth much effort to succeed because of the many-faceted win...for your students, their parents, you, your program, and the school.

—*community*

Establishing relationships with people in the school community is much less clear-cut than those I have already discussed. There are many different configurations of communities. I can't presume to know them all. In fact, I've taught in an inner city for twenty-five years and have probably got some preconceptions that wouldn't work in an upscale neighborhood. Knowing this limitation on my part, I would just like to suggest some places where relationship is possible and/or worthwhile and some ideas on how to create positive interactions.

Elementary and junior high schools that feed into your high school:
- Host tournaments for junior high schools
- Perform children's theatre (tour it sometimes and other times have the junior high students come to your auditorium)
- Do videotapes touting your program for the schools to show at their leisure
- Send your students to give talks about what it's like to come to high school

Local businesses, banks, fast-food places, groceries:
- Put up fliers advertising your shows

- Ask for paid advertisements in your play programs then comp the advertisers
- Take mimes out to perform at holiday or festival times   in hospitals, homes for the retired or handi-capped, and drug rehab centers
- Send student speakers to give informative talks or perform monologues

It's good to do some kinds of community outreach. Generally, you will have some performances that can travel, such as mimes, small shows, oral interpretations. Create opportunities for your students to go out into the community in positive ways, so that they can get more experience in performance and so that you can increase good will for your program and for your high school.

—saying thanks

This may be a little, insignificant thing. Or, it may turn out to be the only important thing I say in this chapter: Send thank you notes. Send personal notes of thanks at the end of the school year to the people who have helped you...secretaries, custodians, other teachers, whomever.

Also, get in the habit of dashing off short thank you notes when people do nice things along the way. For example, if an administrator takes time out of his busy schedule to attend a rehearsal, whether you've invited him or not, send a thank you note.

Involve your students. Let them send thank you notes to teachers who have brought in old clothes for the costume closets or janitors who have carried tables for you.

These little acts of kindness will work miracles in creating good will for you and your program. They will teach your students good manners, too. Here again...win/ win.

—school consciousness

The school has a consciousness, an entity, a "beingness." It has a level of functioning that allows teaching and learning, but also gives support, provides choice, exerts control, gives pleasure, hurts, and heals. All of these functions cross over job description lines. A secretary can be the greatest influence on a student. A student can give the greatest kindness to a teacher. All of the people in the school function across boundaries.

In other words, a school is no different from any other place, be it home, business, or institution. It's a place where people come together and live a great part of their lives. Everybody is important in a school community, from the yardman who picks up trash after lunch to the valedictorian of the senior class. Keep that awareness of the value of all the people, and you'll do fine and be appreciated by all.

CHAPTER 3

Starting a Speech Team

Whether you are starting a speech team in a school where none existed before or taking over an existing team, startup is essentially the same. Attending to the details of setting up a team will result in a positive ongoing experience for you and your team members and can also set a professional tone for future years.

—*governance for competition*

Generally there is a governing body for speech competition, i.e., the National Federation Interscholastic Speech and Debate Association division for your state. Some one in the front office of your school has charge of the competitive activities, probably an assistant principal. You, as a newly hired speech coach, may or may not have been invited to the opening meeting of the coaches on campus, since there isn't a ball involved in speech competition.

     If no one contacts you the first week of school, it's a good idea to find the assistant principal with jurisdiction over coaches, introduce yourself, and ask if you are a part of his/her operation.

—tournament rules book

Once you've identified the supervisory person on your campus, ask for the speech tournament rules book, which is produced by the state governing body. This book will contain a calendar of contests for the current year, general rules for each category of competition, and a listing of the coaches who currently hold offices in the state organization. Read this book from cover to cover, so you won't get any surprises when you start taking kids to tournaments....like a requirement that scripts for orations must be turned in to the tournament director.

The tournament rules book is very important to your day-to-day operation If you can't find a copy of it on your own campus, call another school in your city or district and ask to speak to the speech coach. You might find your answers quickly and easily, and you'll probably establish a contact that will quickly turn into a friendship when you go out on the tournament circuit.

—first team meeting

Next you're ready to find some interested students to participate. It's good to start setting up your team in the second or third week of school because students are generally enthusiastic when school starts and are willing to make a commitment to extra-curricular activities. The date of the first tournament of the year might also help you decide when to put out a call for students. Because students are more likely to attend in the middle of the week, pick a Tuesday, Wednesday, or Thursday, at noon, after school, or during an activity period. Make announcements on the P. A. system and put up some fliers on campus to advertise the first meeting of the speech team.

It's good to outline a calendar of speech tournaments for the year. You might even put that on paper for the students to see, so they and their parents can plan other activities around tournaments. However, don't expect team members to remember all the dates. The chances are ninety-nine out of a hundred that some of them are going to realize they've got a dentist appointment or find out they have to help their dad put a new roof on the house. If you're in the inner city, some are likely just to not make the van because they've overslept or there's no one at home to bring them to the school.

This is where your attitude comes in. You can spin your wheels by getting angry at these students, or you can know it will happen and remain unruffled. Of course, remaining unruffled does not imply that you won't let the kids have it on Monday with a good, long lecture on fulfilling their responsibilities to the team, to the school, and to themselves.

You can project as many tournaments as you feel you can attend, given your other responsibilities at the school. Try to stick to the calendar you've set for the first year. In the second year, you'll have a much more realistic view of how many tournaments are the right number for you and your team.

—*your predecessor's influence*

If you are following another speech coach from the year before, some of the students from that coach's team will want to participate. Some will refuse because their loyalty will remain totally with the old coach, and they'd rather give up competition than work with a new coach. That's okay for you. Whether you have carry-over students or not, you're basically going to have to build your own team and your own relationships with your team members.

It could happen that you have a carry-over student or two who are pushy and want to run the team themselves (like the old coach did) in order to perpetuate the illusion that the old coach is still there. I think these are the students who need you most because they've made a big emotional investment in their old coach; they're angry because he/she left; they feel deserted and are probably grieving. Take the time to nurture these students with a little extra care; then one of two things will happen. They will become your friends and work for the good of the team or they will quit and go out for the tennis team. Either way, you and they will be all right.

Know that you are in a cross-over period, and you are going to win. You will eventually have the loyalty and cooperation of your team members. That's the way of things because the students need you as their coach.

—*coaching*

Quality, self-discipline, and responsibility—those are the values you'll teach something about on speech team. It's good for you to know what they are for you, and your team members will quickly come to your level and accept your value system. It's also important to remember that you have the ability to make your students feel very guilty, so try to show your affection for them and your confidence that they can develop the qualities needed for good competitive work.

Individual coaching sessions of one half hour to an hour each are good to start new team members out. You might want to require that each new team member have two or three such sessions with you before competing in the first tournament. It's good training for young people to make appointments with you and learn to keep them. If you do make that a requirement, remember that you will also need to enforce it...sometimes not an easy choice. If a student has attended two coaching sessions and ditched one, for example, you might lose face with the student if you let him or her go to tournament anyway. On the other hand, you might let that student compete and do poorly with the hope that he or she will learn the value of coaching sessions. Enforcing rules is always a judgment call with high school students.

Later coaching sessions can be very profitably done using older team members to coach younger ones. You might do this in a group situation if you have enough space, outside or in the auditorium, for instance. If your classroom is your only space, you might want to have each competitor practice before you and the other team members, then offer critique to each in turn.

Add a festive flavor to the evening before tournament. Provide snacks or a pitch-in supper in combination with group coaching sessions. Also, going to someone's home for this last session helps to create a team spirit. You might offer your own home from time to time. Team members will probably volunteer their homes, too. This is great because parents become involved with your team. If you are planning to go to a parent's home, call in advance to verify arrangements and, of course, afterwards to say thanks.

Some combination of these coaching arrangements will work for you, but it might take you a while to find out which is best. In addition, you'll probably discover that a procedure will work well one year and not another. The important thing is for each competitor to get individual critique and encouragement to be psychologically ready for competition.

—paperwork and insurance coverage

There is very little commonality among schools about what paperwork is required, regulations about budget or availability of money for your team, or even transportation of your team. The only common thread, it seems to me, is that all three will have to be handled in order to get your team to the first tournament. Once that is accomplished, these concerns should diminish rapidly.

In general, you'll need some kind of permission from parents to take students off campus. You'll need a clearance from the school, probably in the form of one or more pieces of paper. You will also have to arrange transportation for your team, i.e., ordering a bus, a van, a train, or plane. Try the office or principal that handles student

activities and sports. Secretaries are often the most helpful and thorough source of information since the paperwork you create must be processed by them. The secretary in the activities area is most likely the person who
knows. **Ask to be walked through the paperwork procedure the first time to save yourself a lot of back-
tracking later.**

Though the forms of the paperwork vary, the papers themselves are important because somewhere along
the way they will invoke the school's insurance both for
vehicles and for personal liability. Since you will often
take students off campus, you need both types of coverage. In addition, you need some kind of liability insurance of your own. It can be obtained through joining a
local affiliate of the National Education Association or the
American Federation of Teachers. The insurance can
sometimes be obtained as an add-on to a homeowners insurance policy. Don't neglect this detail for your personal
security.

—*eligibility*

Most states have eligibility rules for competition. For example, a student may be required to prove he is passing
four or five classes in order to compete. It's your responsibility to understand what these rules are and enforce
them for your team. Call the principal in charge of
coaches. If he doesn't know, then call the office of the
state's interscholastic association. Don't neglect this detail because you could put your students in the awkward
position of being disqualified from a tournament.

Once you know the eligibility rules, devise a reporting form for your team members to carry to their teachers to indicate pass/fail status. Your school probably already has established rules about how often this must be done; the rules vary from once a week to once a semester. Just take the prevailing trend and go with it and have an awareness that this will change often. Administrators, parents, legislators...just about everybody has an opinion on student eligibility; thus the frequently changing rules.

For you the eligibility is a minor annoyance to process. There may be times, on the other hand, that enforcing it will be painful. Imagine the talented sophomore girl you have who practices her interpretation piece faithfully but can't pass algebra. It will probably fall to you to tell her she can't go to tournament....a poignant part of forensics coaching.

—funding your team

If you're lucky, your school has a budget for forensics. Such budgets often pay for tournament entry fees, buses, and supplies, such as debate materials, play scripts, and stopwatches. Unfortunately many schools do not have such budgets, and it will be up to you and your team to earn money to pay your expenses.

There are many ways students can earn money on campus. These include car washes, bake sales, candy sales, and product sales (such as calendars, key rings, and Christmas candles). Sometimes it's possible to create a parent booster club to offset some of this fund-raising responsibility. If you want to try to start a parent group, discuss it with your team members and set a plan of action. Often a parent of a devoted speech team member will be willing to spearhead such an effort. Nothing can be harmed by trying, but be willing to wash some cars the first year anyway.

—*tournament day*

A lot of preparation has gone into the first tournament of the year: start up plans, searching for materials, coaching sessions, probably some steps and missteps. But, let's assume you got the bus ordered, got the entry sent in on time, and most of the kids made it to the school before the scheduled departure. That's a lot of assuming, but it mostly happens.

The ride to the first tournament is generally a very happy time, full of enthusiasm and excitement. Upon your arrival at the tournament site, perhaps even before you leave the bus, hold a team meeting to cover last-minute details, set the standards for behavior, and build team spirit.

Standards for behavior should be brief but pointed. You expect the students to behave as young adults in such a manner as to make them outstanding representatives of their school. You need to say this in as much detail as seems appropriate. Certainly you want to tell them lunch plans and that you expect them all to return to the bus at the end of the tournament day. **Be sure you have all of their home phone numbers with your entry blank so you can call home if anything inappropriate happens.** If the students know you have their home phone numbers, you've mostly solved your discipline problems anyway. The truth is that generally of the students already know what is expected in the way of behavior. After all, they've been in school for at least 8 years and know what teachers expect. Trust that the kids really want to compete and have a good time, and that's what usually happens.

Once in a while something unpleasant occurs, perhaps a student goes home without letting you know and you're left at the end of the day uncertain about his or her whereabouts. Call home in this circumstance and let the parent know your concern. The whole team will know about this phone call, eliminating many future phone calls. In addition, you will create a lot of good public relations with the parent, who probably knows other parents on the team. Occasionally, students have a more difficult problem. It's good to have the home phone numbers at such times. When in doubt, phone the parents.

Make an effort to create team spirit before the opening round of the first tournament. Perhaps a handshake will do the job. Some people use energy circles. Others do a school cheer or chant. A mascot, such as a stuffed animal, might work. Some type of team bonding is good. If you are uncertain as to what procedure would work for your students, ask them what they would like, either on the day of the first tournament or in advance. Then do it at the first tournament and at others. A little ritual helps build team spirit.

One word about lunch. Until you know your team very well, be sure to have lunch with them on tournament days. Strange as it may seem to someone like you, there are parents who send their kids off on 12-hour tournament days with no money. It's very awkward for the students, and they will often try to hide the fact, so be on the lookout for comments like, "I'm just not hungry today" or "I'm on a diet." Those are likely covers for the fact that a student has no money. Maybe you can arrange to have some slush fund money from your carwashes to cover this contingency. Or, you may just budget a few dollars to be spent on lunches. If this is a major problem, you might consider lunch as a benefit of going to tournament and include it in your fundraising budget.

—*judging*

Sometimes tournament directors provide their own judges. At most tournaments, however, you will be required to provide judges. Certainly serve as a judge yourself. That helps you to see the quality of the competition for your students, as well as allowing you to see the kinds of material often used in tournament. If you need to provide more judges than yourself, ask an English teacher from your school, or perhaps a parent who is well educated. If you are taking over an established team, you might ask your senior members to recommend graduates who might be interested in judging.

It's considered good form on the tournament circuit to provide qualified judges, so make an effort. If you have trouble doing so, be sure to spend some time in the judges' lounge at the tournament. Get acquainted with the other coaches and judges and ask for their help. Know that people who are already on the circuit really enjoy helping someone new to get started. They get a chance to show off their knowledge and be a good Samaritan at the same time. That's great for them and for you.

—recruiting

Team building is an ongoing part of coaching. Involve your present team members in the recruiting process; they are often more effective recruiters than you. Here are some suggestions for finding new team members:

Go into classrooms, such as other speech classes, English classes, social studies classes, or home bases/ homerooms. Make brief, upbeat presentations about the values of being on a speech team, i.e., honing communication skills, making friends, building a college résumé, etc. You might, with a little advance planning through the teachers whose classrooms you visit, plan to give students a demonstration: Send team members out prepared to deliver their oration, duo acting piece, or interpretation piece.

Another idea for exposing the student body to your team members' performances is to ask for time at an assembly. Introduce your present team members and perform some selections. Cheerleaders and student government members are often very supportive of team efforts. They are accustomed to doing so for athletic teams. If they have not traditionally supported speech team at your school, suggest that the team really needs their support and ask for it. You might find this approach surprisingly successful.

This same approach can be useful in the junior high schools that feed into your high school. Take a cadre of your team members and go recruiting at the junior highs. A successful assembly might be mounted as a joint effort with your high school's drama, music, and dance teachers.

Another recruiting avenue is the counselors at your school. They often are influential in helping students choose classes as well as extra-curricular activities. Make sure each counselor has correct information about your program in writing every semester.

—out-of-town trips

Hopefully you have taken your students to one or two successful local tournaments before you undertake an out-of-town trip. You will certainly feel more confident if you have. It's important to know your students before you take them on overnight stays. It's also a lot more complicated to plan, of course, because you will have to secure lodging accommodations, do an itinerary, and send a letter to parents informing them of the plans.

Students love to go on overnights out of town. There's an illusive atmosphere of excitement outside parental control. Certainly they want to compete and they appreciate you for taking them, but you've got to know that they can get crazy in a heartbeat.

You will want the experience of the overnighter to be a good one, and you also want to keep your own sanity. It would be good to get a couple of extra hours of sleep the night before you go because the chances are pretty good that you will be up late. Kids don't seem to sleep at all on overnighters, and the most exhilarating part of the trip is getting to see team members of the opposite sex after midnight.

Be clear about the behavior you expect of them, and be honest about what you're personally willing to enforce. If you say they have to be in their rooms by 10:00 p.m. or they'll be sent home, then you've got to be willing to call their parents and put them on a bus for home if you find them in the motel snack bar at 2:00 a.m. Here again, the kids already know how they should behave. It's just that the temptation to misbehave increases away from home. Try to have a good attitude and emphasize the reason you're on the trip. Keep the tournament in their minds as much as you can. Do bed checks. And send somebody home if you have to, but don't lose faith in the majority of your students. They may be rowdy, but they're basically good.

One more tip on this subject: if it's possible to take along extra chaperones, do. You might find a willing parent or set of parents. Perhaps your own spouse would be willing...other teachers maybe. More adults along will help temper the students' behavior and will certainly make the trip more relaxing and enjoyable for you. Finally, here's this about it: out-of-town trips are a part of your job description, so make them as good for yourself and your team as possible.

—winning and losing

As a coach it's a real joy for you to see your students win in tournament...to see your hard work pay off. They are happy, and you are happy. That's a time for rejoicing.

Pizza parties and hugs are probably in order. Losing, however, is a bit touchier. Following are some reasons why students lose in tournament and possible responses you might make to them:

Students have not performed up to potential: Suggest they work harder and have more coaching sessions.

Students have performed up to potential: Suggest they find new material or change to another event.

There is a point in competition where, all things being equal like talent and material, the win or loss turns on judge's preference, perhaps something so small as the innuendo of a voice or the color of a dress, or whether the judge prefers Tennessee Williams to Arthur Miller. Suggest that, no matter how wonderful all the competitors are, it's the judge's responsibility to declare a winner. Thus all other students will end up losers in that round. Students who are talented and genuine competitors need to realize this truth and be able to rise above it. On the other hand, qualifying for out-rounds is a praise-worthy achievement.

A very important part of the competitive process is in the honing of one's individual communicative and performance skills. That happens whether the competitor wins or loses. This is an outcome that students often don't notice. You need to point it out to them, so that they know the truth of the situation...competition is a win/win situation, not a win/lose situation. If you can impart this truth to your students, you will have equipped them with a tool for living that far exceeds their ability to win a trophy.

—publicizing your team

On the first school morning after tournament, summarize your team's activities for the PA announcements. You can vary your approach: have students read the announcements sometimes; you do it sometimes; and, if some students do outstanding work in competition, ask a principal to read the announcement. That lends a certain class to the achievement.

If there are display cases, kiosks, or bulletin boards available to you on campus, put your students' awards or trophies in them for the student body to see. If you are concerned about their being damaged or stolen, simply put the announcements up, printed or typed on colorful paper.

Try to get your team's accomplishments printed in the school newspaper, even if it's just a news item that they attended a tournament. Doing this might mean you or a team member will have to write a press release each time. Hopefully, your school newspaper will assign a reporter to the speech team's beat. If not, you might make the suggestion. It is important to get the news out to the school that the speech team is competing. That builds public relations and entices future team members.

Outstanding wins on the part of your team might prompt you to write a press release to the local newspapers. Actually, press releases are easy to do, take just a few minutes, and cost only the price of a first class stamp. The return, if they are published, can be enormous to you in team building and public relations for your team and for your school.

Another approach toward publicity is to publish a newsletter for parents, students, and teachers where you and your team write news briefs about your team's activities. Whatever approach you take, it is important to publicize your activities.

Also, be sure there is a page in the school yearbook for speech team. If that has not been a pattern in the past at your school, invest in a lunch with the yearbook advisor and suggest it. Long-term gains come to the team that is chronicled in the yearbook.

—*hosting tournaments*

Don't, your first year! You might want to hold onto this book until you do feel comfortable enough to host a tournament. There is a chapter on it.

—*your coaching stipend*

Some school districts provide an extra stipend for coaching forensics; some consider it a part of the speech teacher's job. However that is for you, you probably knew it when you hired into the job. Just a word of caution: If you are supposed to receive a stipend, check the math on your paycheck to make sure you get it.

Though the financial rewards for coaching a speech team may not make the payments on a Mercedes, the psychic rewards might. Through the bonding that comes from teamwork, quality friendships are formed, yours with your students and your students' with each other.

Speech training is one of the most tangible gifts a teacher can give a student. Over the years, it has been the speech students who have returned to tell me their training has had a major impact on their career achievements and their personal self-confidence.

CHAPTER 4

Directing the First Show

If a potential Matt Damon or Gwyneth Paltrow show up at auditions, and they might, your show will be a lot better. But, the goal of the after-school production is not to create such acting giants. Teaching love of the theatre and personal responsibility...those are worthwhile goals you can accomplish...and for which your students will be grateful. Your effort to help them perform the best show they are capable of performing is your gift to your students.

—your role: director, producer, technical director

If you are working in a large high school performing arts program, you may be a director, producer, or technical director for your first high school show. In that case, you probably will have more seasoned teachers to share with and get guidance from. However, many new teachers find themselves in small drama programs or are in fact hired to create them.

If that's your situation, it's important for you to define your role for yourself. You are first and foremost the director. If you have a talent for or experience in the other two areas, find two staff members who are looking for an extra-curricular assignment to be your producer and tech director. Your leadership based on your own background should get the job done reasonably well. If you can't locate such faculty members, entrust the jobs to two senior drama students. That will require more leadership and guidance from you, but it is necessary to take such a focus. You need to be the director to keep all of the responsibilities in tact, though you may feel that you are doing far more than was usually expected of directors in the college you attended.

The critical thing is for you to establish yourself in the leadership role, with primary responsibility for directing and secondary responsibility for producing and tech directing. Students will expect and accept you in that role. Be prepared to spend much time in all areas of production. Be prepared to take costumes home and sew them or to come in on the Saturday before the show to paint sets.

Having everything work when the curtain goes up is, finally, your responsibility. Whatever it takes to get there is what you have to do. Later you'll have time to reflect on which students contribute, what jobs you can slight, and what jobs require your full attention. If you get a little flaky toward the end of the rehearsal schedule, just say so in plain words like, "I'm sorry I yelled at you. I'm just worried that the show won't be good," or "I guess I've got a little stage fright too." Your young actors will appreciate your honesty and feel that they are a part of something with you.

One of the greatest values of after-school productions is the closeness and team spirit that develop when you and the students are working together for a common goal. In fact, this is where the relationships are forged that will allow you to have positive impact on your students' lives and enrich your own. Those warm fuzzies are worth working for, and there is definitely a lot of work to it. So, here goes.

—*your predecessor's influence*

If you are stepping into an ongoing theatre program, you may find yourself dealing with some angry or hurt students whose loyalty is to your predecessor. I make some suggestions on how to handle this problem in the chapter entitled Starting a Speech Team. You might want to read through that.

—*production costs*

Producing a show in high school involves some costs: royalties and scripts, set and costume rental or purchase, props, makeup, tickets, programs, perhaps some publicity. Shows vary in cost from a few hundred to many thousands of dollars.

It's important that you know whether or not you will receive a budget from the school to pay for your productions, whether box office sales are expected to finance them, or whether you will have to sell candy and do car-washes to make ends meet.

Don't leave yourself open to any surprises in this area. Find out where the money is going to come from. Ask the person who hired you, your department chair, or the administrator in charge of activities.

—*selecting a play*

There's no "right" script for your first production. A great many will do nicely. Here are some ideas to consider.

What type of community are you working in? What shows have been produced there in the past? Were they well received? Talk to some older teachers and/or some seniors to find out. You might want to check through your school's yearbooks to become familiar with the kind of shows your faculty and student body have been exposed to. It's possible you might want to improve the quality of choices, but in any case it's good to know what's been done. It's also very smart to get to know the yearbook sponsor because a lot of the ongoing publicity for your program appears in the pages of the school yearbook.

Choose a cast size smaller than the number of students you think might tryout. If you honestly don't know whether there will be ten or eighty, choose two shows, one with a big cast and one with a small one. Tell the students you will make a decision on which show to produce after the audition.

Pick a show you like, perhaps one you worked on in high school or college. You don't have to reinvent the wheel on the first show. Once you're feeling comfortable as a high school director, your creativity will blossom quickly.

The script should have good dramatic values, so you will feel confident that your vehicle will help your students get a quality theatrical experience. Samuel French's catalog contains a list of most often produced high school plays. The International Thespian Society magazine produces a similar list.

Trust that whatever choice you make for your first script will probably work out okay if you've followed even some of these guidelines... and avoided profanity and sex. Some things never change!

—directorial concept

Create a clear concept in your own mind of the main idea you want to get across with the show. The theme of the play is basic to the directorial concept. This idea may seem elementary to you, but it will not be to your students. It's important to communicate to them the message your production will carry to the audience. Talk about it. Work to incorporate your concept into all facets of the production. How is the message amplified by the costumes? How do the lights and sound contribute to the main theme?

Ask your students to help you with this process. By doing so you will engage their minds in the dramatic values of the production and help them see the historical

and societal value of the theatre they do, i.e., what statement are we making to our community by doing this
show? What statement do we want to make?

—auditions

Advertise your auditions through whatever means are
most common in your school: the P A system, the school
newspaper, fliers, posters...any or all. Make sure the word
gets out for at least a week before the day of auditions. If
you feel a callback day will be needed, include that in the
opening announcements. If you don't know whether call-
backs will be necessary, make the decision at the audition.
Be sure to state the kind of audition you're doing. If you
use a prepared audition, make multiple copies in advance
so that students may come by and pick them up before the
audition.

　　Also, prepare some kind of audition sheet. Many
drama texts have samples. Make sure you have slots on
the audition sheet for home phone numbers, the daily class
schedule, and space for notes. Once auditions are under-
way, you may have some difficulty remembering which
student goes with which name. If you have an audition
sheet, you can make notes for your own use, such as "tall
blonde in green blouse." That will make casting easier
later.

　　There is no right kind of audition, prepared or
cold, scripted or improvised. In an ongoing drama program, a variety of auditions is the best experience you can
give your students. For the first show, simply do the kind

of audition you feel most comfortable with. You'll have time to cycle through the others later.

—*creating a rehearsal schedule*

A rehearsal schedule can be as complicated or as simple as you would like to make it. If you have worked with a rehearsal schedule in the past that you liked, use it because that will give you one familiar piece of the production puzzle.

For a full-length show, I reserved eight weeks with four rehearsals per week for two to two and a half hours after school. Here is a format that has worked for me.

Week 1: Cast and crew meeting, read through, block Act 1

Week 2: Crew meetings, run Act 1, block Act 2

Week 3: Run Acts 1 and 2, reblock as necessary

Week 4: Off book on Act 1, run Act 2

Week 5: Off book on Act 2, run both acts

Week 6: Start props, see costumes, polish acting, begin publicity

Week 7: Start sound effects, sets, lights, polish acting

Week 8: Full technical and dress rehearsals

Think through all of the technical aspects of the show and stipulate deadlines for your tech people on the rehearsal schedule. That way all of your cast and crew will have a common time frame for production.

Don't be afraid to vary the schedule if you need to; however, if you are going to cancel a rehearsal, it's good to let parents know. Kids have a way of getting in trouble when the drama coach thinks they've gone home and the parents think they're at rehearsal.

If you get very far behind, on the other hand, you may have to add some evenings or Saturdays, especially to finish up tech. Oftentimes turnout for such extra events is poor. It's more productive to schedule more rehearsal and tech time than you think you'll need and spend the time polishing.

—*eligibility*

If you're lucky, your state won't require eligibility for participation in a play, but check with your activities office to make certain. If there is an eligibility requirement, refer to the section on eligibility in the chapter entitled Starting a Speech Team.

—*permissions and royalties*

Whenever you keep students after school, you usually need some kind of parent permission slip. Check with your activities principal to find out what is standard at your school. It's a good practice to send the form home with a letter to the parents, including the rehearsal schedule. If they sign the permission slip and send it back, you can be pretty certain they've seen the rehearsal schedule. That should cut down on a lot of confusion later.

Royalties for any published play must be paid in advance of the performance. The amounts for a first performance are generally a few dollars higher than the second or third performances. When you order a set of acting scripts from a play catalog, the publisher will send you a form for performance royalties. Don't neglect to pay these royalties. Some companies do check to see if high schools and community colleges are fudging on their royalties. Also, you'll probably want to teach your students integrity in doing the business of the theatre, which includes paying royalties.

—*treatment of scripts*

Most scripts can be performed as they are written; and, for the most part, you'll probably want to do that. From time to time, though, you may find that you want to eliminate lines or a scene for an assortment of reasons. Maybe the show is too long, a scene is sexually explicit, the language is too raw, or an actor has trouble with some lines.

Most of the time you can feel comfortable cutting or even piecing together a scene now and then as long as you don't change the intent of the playwright. Once in a while a script will have a warning on the front that it cannot be altered, such as *Our Town* by Thornton Wilder. That is an unusual circumstance, however.

—*crew work*

Get a responsible person, either a faculty member or a top-notch senior to head up your crew work. For the first show, elaborate sets and lighting designs may be too ambitious. It's more important for the students and you to have a good experience than it is to do a technical masterpiece. So, my suggestion is to keep it simple technically.

No matter how simple the show, there are going to be important technical aspects to consider. Seek out help in departments on your campus that might have expertise. For example, if there is a sewing class, the teacher may be happy to have some unusual projects for the sewing students, such as making costumes. Call the woodshop teacher for help in getting wood cut or building needed items, such as platforms. If you want music or some musical sound effects, chat with your music teacher.

Look also at Good Will and Salvation Army stores for cheap props and costumes. If you're lucky, local furniture stores might be interested in loaning props to you in exchange for an ad in your program. Some or all of these liaisons may work out; if they do not, you'll have to rely on the ingenuity of your students and yourself.

Parents are also often a good source of help on technical work. Ask in rehearsal if there are parents who can sew costumes, build platforms, or bring in large props. Certainly having parents involved enhances and builds a sense of community around your program. It's also good for the show, good for the parents, and good for the students…a can't-miss situation.

—*rehearsals*

Start and end rehearsals on time as much as possible. As with so many other aspects of high school teaching, students will respond to your expectations. If you start rehearsal late, they'll arrive late. If you remind them to be on time and start promptly, they'll develop the habit of being on time.

Discipline at rehearsal is not the same as in the regular classroom. The rules can be relaxed to good advantage. For example, in the classroom you might expect students to ask permission to go to the bathroom or to talk with someone. Those permissions are not necessary at rehearsal, as long as the actor makes his or her cue.

Major infractions must be treated as they would be during the school day. For example, if a student arrives at rehearsal inebriated, the same disciplinary actions should be taken, whatever those are for your school. If that involves writing, a referral, then do so. You might also consider dropping the student from the show altogether, for the good of the whole cast. Even though you might be required to take the student back into the classroom after punishment, you have more personal choice in an after-school activity. If in doubt on these areas, talk with one of the older coaches and find out the informal standards for your school.

You also should address the matter of actors who fail to attend rehearsal. Whatever rules you set or enforce will depend in part on your personality. One technique I have used is to say each actor has one ditch but all other absences have to be excused. Another method is to allow three absences for whatever reasons. Or, you might require all absences to be excused. Then again, you may not allow any absences.

There's no best way. Attendance patterns in your school will impact the situation. The number of students you find willing to be understudies will also impact the situation. Understudies tend to put pressure on the talent to have good attendance, especially if they believe you will replace them.

Whatever standards you choose for attendance at rehearsal, remember that leniency is an option for you. If you feel that an actor has a valid reason for not attending rehearsal or a problem that is overwhelming him or her, a reaction that often happens with teenagers, then by all means be lenient. But, remember that your primary responsibility is to the whole cast and to the show. Don't put them in jeopardy. As much as you might hate to do it, you may find that you have to replace your most talented performer for the good of the whole group.

On the other hand, don't allow the students to rule you in this arena. A few may from time to time develop the belief that they are critical to the show and that you'll have to cancel it without them. That's a dangerous belief for a high school student to have. Even though you might feel panicky about kicking a kid out of a show in the last week or two before a performance, you may find you have to do it. If, at that point, he or she is not coming to rehearsal, he or she is not an actor, not a trouper. You need to find someone else, even if that person carries a book through the performance.

Actually, it's amazing what a costumer or stage manager can do at the last minute if you allow him or her the chance at a part. The replacement might surprise you by memorizing all the lines, never missing a cue, and carrying off the part better than the self-centered teenager you originally cast could have done.

The important idea for you to remember is that you are their drama teacher. Your job is to teach them theatre

and self-responsibility. Once that prime directive is ful-filled, of course you want to do the best show you can. But don't sacrifice quality teaching for a quality show. In the long run, the most positive learning that comes out of a show might very well be the turn-around in attitude of the student you kicked out. You really never know for sure how things are going to turn out, so the best you can do is always maintain your integrity and teach the kids they have to come to rehearsal and do their best in per-formance. That's the name of the game of teaching.

—*house management and publicity*

Ultimate responsibility for publicity, tickets, and programs all are a part of your role as director of the high school show. Here again, if you can involve another faculty member or a responsible senior, your burden can be con-siderably lightened in this area. Whoever does the tasks, here they are:

Publicize your show in all the areas that apply for you: in your school, in the school district, and in the com-munity. Think of the media available in each of those ar-eas and use the ones that are free.

- School: Intercom, fliers, posters, assembly teasers, press release to newspaper or a reporter with the drama beat (If there isn't one, suggest it to the newspaper sponsor.)
- District: Newsletters, fliers and complimentary tickets to drama departments in other schools
- Community: Press releases to the local newspa-pers, fliers in store windows and/or parking lots,

teasers in the local supermarkets on Saturday morning or in hospitals or other public service places, complimentary tickets to all the people who helped you with the show, even a little bit.

Tickets must be ordered, printed, and distributed for sale. Cast and crew members might participate in advance sale of tickets. There's good and bad in that technique; you might sell more tickets, but some students will lose their tickets or fail to turn in the money for them. In fact, an occasional enterprising soul has done a sturdy little side business in "lost" show tickets.

The program information must be collected, typed or keyed into a computer, and printed. In the process you might engage a promising art student in designing an attractive program cover. That's good PR and is also good for the self-esteem of the art student. Be sure to check the copy of the program for typographical errors more than once, no matter who prepares it. Take a few minutes at a rehearsal for the cast and crew to check the program mockup, too. There's something a little demoralizing about rehearsing for eight weeks and then being listed as Max, instead of Mark, in the program.

Be sure you have arranged with your school bookstore or other money-handling agency to have a cashbox and change available for performance nights. Also, an hour before show time you need a trustworthy person in the ticket booth, preferably another faculty member, a trusted senior, or even your significant other; but, it can't be you. You have to be backstage on performance nights at least until the curtain goes up. Then it would be great for you to be in the audience to take some pride in your accomplishment, if that's possible.

Arrange in advance for some students, maybe from your drama class, to be ushers. If you want to sell refreshments at intermission, the ushers can handle that, too. It's very pleasant for the audience to have refreshments, but only do it if you've got someone you can trust in the box office. Otherwise, it's just too much for you to run back and forth from the lobby to backstage during performance and intermission.

—recruiting

The best kind of recruiting is a good show, well produced, well publicized, and well received. Other students who see the show will often want to become involved. There are some other strategies to help build a drama program or increase the number of students who audition, whichever might be your goal.

One good way to increase exposure to plays is a part of publicity for the show you're currently producing: try to get a slot on an all-school assembly to perform a teaser of your show. Or, volunteer your actors to do short skits on assembly subjects. You can have traveling minstrels, mimes, or simply actors in costumes walk around the campus to advertise a show or to participate in other school activities, such as parent nights or money-raising bazaars.

Another very effective recruiting tool is the touring show, particularly if that tour goes to elementary or junior high schools which feed into your high school. This could be done as a children's theatre performance or as an assembly in a joint project with music, dance, and speech. Or, this assembly could go to the junior high schools to showcase after-school activities, such as sports, clubs, and activities like theatre. In any event, sixth, seventh, and eighth graders will be your actors in a couple of years; and they'll remember when your show came to their elementary or junior high school.

See also the chapter on Starting a Speech Team for related recruiting ideas. Any time you can join up with another teacher for recruiting purposes, do so. It can only work to your good in building your program.

—alternatives to a main stage show

Although the main stage show is the backbone of the drama program in any high school, there are some viable alternatives that you might want to consider...for many reasons. One reason is simply variety of artistic expression. Or, if you're in the inner city, you may find getting your actors to rehearsal after school is all but impossible because of other stresses on their lives. Whatever the reason, here are some other ideas for giving your students performance opportunities:

Tours of elementary or junior high schools, local hospitals, homes for the elderly, banks, or any other group of institutions. Choose a short show that can travel with costumes and a minimum of set pieces. The choice of show will probably relate to the audience you're going after, i.e., *Cinderella* for elementary schools or *A Christmas Carol* for banks. Write a letter introducing the idea to all of the individual schools, hospitals, homes, or other institutions. Lists are easy to come by. Look in the white pages of the telephone directory. In the letter, describe your show and say that you are willing to do it free or for a certain fee, what the size demands are for the playing space, and that you will phone them in a couple of weeks. Then, call in two weeks, and you'll probably get a lot of takers.

Feature films are an exciting alternative, particularly if your school has an audio-visual person who likes to do projects with students or if you just have a friend with a camcorder. There are film scripts available through play publishing catalogs. You can rehearse, then put each segment on film. If you want to get into editing, it's often possible to rent an editing machine. Public access television is a possible medium for such a project as well. Cable stations are required by law to provide public access, and they are happy to work with you. A public showing of your work in the auditorium for parents and community to see is appropriate; after all, we're all used to paying to see movies. Besides the delight of sitting in the audience with their parents, cast and crew members can have personal copies of the video made for a keepsake or raw footage for a demonstration tape for your career-oriented students...many bonuses for a film project.

Exchange programs with other drama teachers might include teaming up with the drama teacher in another school to produce a show together. You could perform the show at both schools. This is a very broadening activity for your students; and it is interesting news, so you can often get city newspaper coverage that might not be available for a show you're doing at your own school. Another turn an exchange might take would be to simply perform your show at the other campus and have the other school's actors perform at yours.

—after-school relationships

The shows you direct and produce after school are the soul of your program. Mutual respect and warm friendships often develop in this atmosphere. You will find students beginning to trust you at a personal level more than they ever do in the regular classroom.

Over the course of a thirty-year career, I have maintained contact with many of my former students. They have become lifetime friends. None of those friendships grew out of classroom work—only out of shows...good work done together as friends.

The relationships you develop with students in the after-school program will have more of the flavor of actor and director relationships. The beginnings of professionalism are fostered here.

Young actors learn not only to come to rehearsal on time but also to revere the creative spirit within them. They will learn to respect the teacher's creativity as well and depend on it to give their talent its outlet.

The shows you do after school take the most time and effort. But, make no mistake: There will be students in your cast and crew who would have dropped out of school had you not put out an audition call. It is here that

you will know you're making a difference in your students' lives.

The care and nurturing of young actors and theatre technicians is a worthy goal and productive for society.

Additionally, you have the privilege of sharing your students' problems and concerns in an atmosphere that inspires confidence and trust...something all human beings need, not just young people.

I hope someday you can say as I have said that I am blessed by God to be a drama teacher.

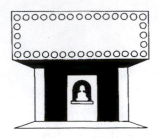

CHAPTER 5

Running an Auditorium

Whether or not it's a part of your job description to run the auditorium, if you are the drama teacher, the job generally falls to you because no one else on the campus really knows how to do it. Actually, it's to your advantage to run the auditorium because more will go your way in the building if you are there running it than if someone else runs it and you have to reserve it for rehearsals.

—stewardship

An auditorium is a building with lots of steel, tall and drafty passage ways, expensive equipment and drapery. An auditorium is the most complex building on a school campus. An auditorium is a multi-million dollar building created and dedicated to the search for truth through illusion. An auditorium is a public symbol of the desire for community, communication, and the comfort of belonging which springs from their exercise. Forums that decide public policy, shows that capture the imaginations of their auditors, concerts that inspire. Life happens there...the life

of the community of which the school is a critical component. Without the school, the community is irreparably
crippled; without the auditorium, the school is equally so.

Stewardship of an auditorium is a sacred trust.
To keep it running and responsive to the school and community takes time, effort, and devotion. I have had the
unique experience of having loved my auditorium since it
was embryonic. I helped to code its DNA and assisted at
its birth. Now that it is an adult, I have respect for it cou-
pled with the fondness that comes from having nurtured it
through many years of growing up in the school and community it was built to serve.

There have been many days when I felt the weight
of that auditorium like an albatross around my neck, and
I've thought how lovely to be a regular teacher who
teaches five classes and goes home to a patio or television.
But, when I've sat in the audience and listened to the
Phoenix Symphony play from my stage or watched a
show I've worked countless hours to direct or seen an
NBA All-Star give an award to a handicapped kid, I know
I made the right choice.

Caring about the auditorium and keeping it running for the school and the community have been an important part of my job. In fact, when someone wants me
to give to the United Way, I simply smile at the redun-
dancy of the request.

—maintenance and repairs

Although the actual hands-on maintenance and repair of
the building and equipment are not your responsibility,

your supervision of both are essential to the smooth operation of the building. If the ropes on the counter-balance system are fraying or the stage floor needs paint, you are the first one to notice. Then, you'll want to find the proper method for getting the maintenance done.

School systems vary considerably in the way they handle maintenance and repair. You may have a budget and the authority to contract with vendors to maintain and repair your equipment. You may be required to work through a department chair or an assistant principal; or, you may have to submit requisitions to a district office to accomplish your objectives.

Whatever the method is in your school, it's important that you understand it thoroughly. Make an appointment with your principal and/or the principal's secretary to go over the details of the methods you need to use to accomplish maintenance and repairs. You will also want to clarify at this time what budget amount you have as well as what the budget covers...maintenance, repair, equipment replacement...all or none of these.

The next step is to get to know the people who will be involved in the maintenance and repair of your building. If there is a custodian assigned to clean the building, meet him or her and have an informal chat about your expectations for the cleanliness of the building and also what the custodian expects of you. Do the same with the head of maintenance. If there are district-level maintenance personnel, as often there are in large school districts, get to know them as well. You may discover some indispensable friends here, such as a sound technician whose job is to maintain your sound equipment or an electrician who services your light board.

—light and sound equipment

This equipment is essential to the smooth running of the building, no matter what group is performing. You have several distinct responsibilities in this area.

First, you need to know how to run your equipment. If there are no manuals available, check first with the head of maintenance of your school. Next, try your district office if your school district is large enough to have a person in charge of equipment repair. As a last resort, call the manufacturer and request a manual.

Whether you've got the manual or not, you will want to spend time figuring out the peculiarities of your system. **Make the operation of the equipment your own.** Otherwise, you won't be able to teach the students how to run it. And, teaching your students how to run the equipment is critical to the operation of the building.

It's also up to you to see that the equipment stays in good repair. That means checking it periodically to make sure everything works. As your students become comfortable with the equipment, they will also let you know when there are problems. Emphasis here is on detection of problems when you are with some drama students setting up for a show. What you want to avoid is finding out that the spotlight is burned out while an assembly is in progress.

You'll probably do specialty light settings and cues for your own shows, but you'll not likely have the time to do so for many of the events in the building. Keep a basic light setting available at all times for assemblies, rentals, and other people's shows, i.e., full, even light across the stage and some cyclorama colors. Also, it's a good idea to teach everyone who is willing to learn how to turn on these settings. Besides your own students, that should include janitors, security guards, assistant principals, other teachers, or anyone else who uses the building or must be there for events.

In summary, treat the light and sound equipment in the auditorium like you do your light and sound equipment at home. If a light bulb is burned out, replace it. If a speaker doesn't work, fix it or replace it. Just stay on top of the situation.

—plumbing

As the drama teacher you probably don't think of yourself as the person in charge of plumbing in your building; but, here's where you might be misjudging the situation. **Schools run on hierarchies.** People are in charge of other people: principals are in charge of teachers, and teachers are in charge of students. People are also in charge of things. The basketball coach is in charge of the gym; the baseball coach is in charge of the diamond; and....you guessed it...the drama teacher is in charge of the auditorium. If you call somebody to come and fix the light board, then you're in charge of the auditorium.

It's a natural progression for you to be in charge of the plumbing. Therefore, if the toilet stops up and water is streaming down the hallway, you'd better phone the head of maintenance or the assistant principal in charge of facilities. Otherwise, it will be on your *head* if the plumbing backs up all over the school.

Just do what is needful to get the problem handled. Don't worry about it or give it excessive weight, like thinking you shouldn't have to do such things because they're not in your job description. Everything having to do with the building is in your job description, whether it's written down or not. The downside of that may be when you're wading through a flooded bathroom. The upside is that you may be consulted on matters of building policies and procedure that can be important to the smooth running of your daily life.

—*safety*

Your students and you have the right to work in a safe environment. Safety standards and inspections are very important to that directive. Most city codes require that schools be inspected for safety violations, and some of the areas to be checked are in the auditorium, such as the fire curtain and the sprinkler system. You will likely not have any responsibility for seeing that those safety checks happen.

Some safety rules, however, are appropriate:

- Students should not load or unload the counter-balance system unless you are present.
- No more than two or three students should be out on the catwalks at the same time.

- Ladders should have safety cages.
- Safety goggles should always be worn when saws are in operation.

You may find other rules necessary. Think through what makes you comfortable in regard to safety rules, so that you won't worry or, more importantly, have any student injuries.

One characteristic that all auditoriums share is that they have a lot of doors. Keeping those doors locked during the school day is important because unsupervised students might get into areas of the building where they could get hurt or do damage. If they do get into the backstage area or the control booths and steal or vandalize something, then you've got a lot of work to do in repair and replacement, not to mention the disciplinary actions you'll probably get involved with in the front office. Also, the school may or may not have the money to cover the losses from vandalism.

One additional problem might be that school insurance policies are not always comprehensive. Once the soundboard was stolen at my school because a repairman left a door unlocked. We had no soundboard in the auditorium for a year and a half because of lean financial times in my school district. It's to your advantage to avoid these situations as much as possible by locking doors.

—scheduling

Scheduling events in the auditorium may be a preset procedure when you arrive at the school. That function may be entirely in the hands of the assistant principal in charge of activities or, more likely, in the hands of the secretary. Or, you might have some say in scheduling. If there is no set procedure for scheduling, you're in luck. Arrange it so that you have final say on who gets to use the building and when. If you do, you can always make sure you have a couple of weeks to put your set up before a show. That's something of a luxury in many schools, but it's still a worthy goal for a drama teacher.

If you can't quite manage to get the final say, at least make sure that you are notified as to who is using the building and when. Otherwise, you're going to have difficulty and frustration in running your own program. Plus, you've got the additional task of providing technical assistance for most of the events that happen in the auditorium, so you'll need to arrange for students who can work.

It is reasonable for you to ask for a copy of any paperwork regarding the reservation of your auditorium. **Insist on it.** Don't provide technical assistance if you don't get such notification. It's sometimes very difficult to achieve this kind of communication, but it's the most basic courtesy that you deserve as the person who is running the building. I hope you never have to do so; but, if you're against the wall, take this book to your front office and have the culprits read this sentence:

THE DRAMA TEACHER MUST RECEIVE NOTIFICATION OF EVERY EVENT SCHEDULED IN THE AUDITORIUM. NO NOTIFICATION...NO LIGHTS...NO SOUND...NO EVENT.

—assemblies

Assemblies are the lifeblood of the school; no one knows why. Certainly they are not good theatre. In fact, they might compete for the worst theatre that will ever get produced on your stage. On the other hand, assembly days infuse the school with vitality. Just knowing there will be an assembly gives your students a buzz all day long. Even though assemblies are a colossal irritation, they serve a very useful purpose for the school in bonding the student body. Therefore, they are an activity you will probably find yourself more involved in than you ever wanted to be.

You will be working with people who know very little about how to do theatre but a great deal about what they want. You will want to determine what it is they need and then do what you can to make that happen. A student government representative might be in charge and tell your drama student to turn off the spotlight because the glare hurts his eyes. He might say that at a rehearsal or during the performance in front of the audience, in which case the light goes out, the audience can't see the performer on stage, and the drama student is angry and embarrassed. A lot of things will happen that you would never allow in your own shows. You just have to learn to live with that. Teach your drama students that they are performing a service for the school and let it go.

There are some things you can do to smooth the assembly. First, establish tech crews from among your drama students. Many of them will volunteer because they can get out of class to run the auditorium equipment. It's a good idea to rotate this duty to some extent so that you've got a number of students who can run the equipment. It's good training for them and eases your mind.

Train a few senior students to function as stage managers for assemblies. You'll be giving them training in accepting responsibility and practice in working with others. Try to create a technical team atmosphere with the light board and sound operators reporting to the stage manager.

Ask for copies of the agenda for yourself and the drama students who will be running the equipment. Read over the agenda to make certain you understand it. If you don't, ask questions. For example, the agenda might say "Band". You might think that means that the band will come on stage to perform. On the other hand, it could mean that the band will come through the audience, requiring that the houselights be turned on...a cue no one thought to say in advance.

Request a rehearsal for each assembly. Even if that means you are only talking through a dry technical rehearsal, at least your drama students will get a sense of what the assembly is supposed to look like. Watching an assembly that has never been rehearsed is depressing. Things always go wrong. I hope you never have to see such a sorry sight. You won't if you tell the people running the assembly that a rehearsal is essential and they believe you. If they don't believe you, then you'll get to see one incredibly bad assembly. Let's just hope there's only one that bad before the message gets out that rehearsals are critical.

Be friendly with the people in charge of the assembly. Offer suggestions about placement of microphones or furniture on stage. Generally, people in charge of assemblies know they don't know what they're doing, and they'll be responsive to your help. With a few well-placed suggestions, you can make an assembly look passable.

It is in your best interest to make assemblies go off as well as you can because you will find yourself being judged for them on campus. Even though you and everyone else knows that assemblies are sponsored by student government, honor society, or "whatsis," people on campus just expect them to look like your shows. In fact, they'll ask you what went wrong when an assembly goes badly. This may seem unfair to you and it is, but that's the way it is, so you'll have to make the best of it.

—your shows, other people's shows, rentals

You were hired to be the drama teacher but everyone sees you as a theatre manager. You are judged more for what happens in the building than you are for the acting and technical skills your students develop or for the quality of your program and productions. I know that's not your priority, and it shouldn't be; but, it's important to know what other people think.

Other people see you as the person running the auditorium. You're their major technical assistant, and they will depend on your expertise to make their shows work.

You will find that you become an ombudsman for the renter or other guest in the building. You may have to phone the custodians to get the air conditioning turned on. You may have to secure keys for the renter. You may have to teach the renter how to run the light board. It's important to keep your "perspectives."

- Perspective 1: See that your sets, props, and costumes are kept secure when other people are in the building.
- Perspective 2: Give guests help, advice, and the work of some of your students, but don't do their show for them. Save your energy for your own show.
- Perspective 3: If they paid money to use the building, be sure that you and the drama students get paid, too.

One additional tip on renters: Chances are your school already has a procedure in place for doing the rentals, including writing the contract and receiving the money. It is appropriate for you to ask where the rental money goes and to ask for some of it for your building if it does not come to you automatically. Light bulbs, gels, and other disposable items in the auditorium should be paid for, at least in part, from rental money because they are partially used up by the renters. If possible, get a procedure instituted so that you can expect some funds to come from rentals on an ongoing basis.

—*your technicians and you*

The young people who serve as your technicians in the building are probably some of the most dedicated students you will ever have. They love to do theatre, and they are invaluable to you, to the school, and to the community. It's important to remember that they have homework to do and family to see. Don't overuse them. A trick here is to train enough students to carry the load, so that you don't burden any particular students.

It's also good to remember that these students will gain reputations in the school as experts in technical theatre. They will take a part of their school identity from that and perhaps for the first time in their young lives receive respect for their accomplishments. That is a very good thing. Encourage others who use the building to rely on your students instead of you. That benefits the others, your students, and you because you personally may get a little more free time.

The flipside is that technicians often get worked pretty hard. Even though others in the school see them as experts, your students can get taken for granted and taken advantage of. They can end up running the light board so many days in a row that they flunk math. It's your job to protect them from that.

Additionally, look for opportunities to honor your drama students who give technical assistance to the school. If there's a student of the month award, nominate them. Give them an award at the end of the year; buy a little trophy and have it engraved "Outstanding Technician." Do take the time to honor these students because without them the auditorium doesn't hum.

Also, honor yourself. Remember that running an auditorium is a difficult, frustrating, and generally thankless job. Also remember that you probably need to do it in order to protect the drama program in your school from the danger of being displaced because of the demands on the building. Buy yourself a trophy, too!

CHAPTER 6

Hosting a Tournament

If you read the chapter on Starting a Speech Team, you know that I advised you to avoid hosting a tournament in your first year of teaching. Given the choice, you probably would not host one because any sensible person knows it's a lot of work. However, one does not always get one's choice in our business. Hopefully, this is your second year of teaching, you're an "old pro" by now, and you just remembered this chapter was in this book you used to refer to last year.

Whatever your particular situation is, you're about to launch into one of the most exciting and demanding duties of your forensics coaching career. Some coaches might laugh at that last line, but I always enjoyed hosting tournaments. It was one of my favorite parts of the job. I hope you will enjoy it, too.

--two keys to a successful tournament

Organization is the first key to a successful tournament. Attention to detail the second.

--what to organize

First, you've got to organize the tournament director...
YOU. Get a notebook or clipboard that is dedicated to the
tournament. A computer disk reserved for tournament use
is a good idea, too, especially if your computer is near
your phone. Start a things-to-do list and update it daily.

Next you've got to organize people, facilities,
time, the paper flow, and the food supply. What follows
is an overview of the tasks involved in conducting a successful tournament. Details will vary from tournament to
tournament, from state to state, and from governing body
to governing body.

Conforming to the particular governing body is
important because the rules and the energy given to enforcing them can be so different. Of the last two tournaments I hosted, one was Arizona State Finals, governed by
the Arizona Interscholastic Association, a limb of the national association. Its tournament rules are very specific,
down to the ways rounds are set and the kind of ballots
you must use. The other tournament I hosted was sponsored by my state's forensic league, a loose affiliation of
speech coaches where rules are less arbitrary and events
are discretionary.

I suggest that you speak directly with the president
of the governing body for your tournament to make certain that you honor the rules already established. Ask for
a printed copy of the rules. Certainly, forensics work is
fluid with rules and category changes. However, your
first tournament is not the place to be creative.

Just getting the tournament going in the traditional manner is taxing enough.

Study the rules book thoroughly, so there are no surprises later. Then, begin your things-to-do list. That list will probably include many of the tasks that follow. In some places I include materials from my own tournaments, which may serve as models for you.

Find some other teachers to assist you. These should be other teachers at your home school or speech coaches from other schools. One adult should be in charge of food for the tournament. One should run registration and the tab room on tournament day. One should run the play competition, if there is one.

—facilities planning

Reserve your entire campus for the time span of the tournament. You'll probably need to obtain permission from your principal to do this. In any case, it's good technique to tell the principal in advance that you are planning to host a tournament and get an informal approval. Then do the appropriate paperwork to clear through the administrative offices.

An aside here is that you can get some free good will for your speech team with the principal. Point out to him or her that students and coaches will be coming from all over the state. This is a prestigious event for a high school. You might even ask your principals to come to the closing assembly and give out awards. That creates a win/win situation for everyone...the principal, the school, your team, the competitors, and you.

Meet with your key school personnel. Early in the planning stages, identify the key people at your school whose functions will be necessary at the tournament. Possible people to invite are: assistant principal in charge of facilities, head of maintenance, head of security, librarian, head of audio-visual services, head of food service, and the teachers/coaches who will be organizing food, the tab room, and the play competition.

The task of organizing the tournament will be much easier if certain details are arranged at this meeting. For example, security or maintenance will unlock doors of classrooms and restrooms at pre-assigned times; maintenance will leave early on Thursday and stay late on Friday, for example, to expedite cleaning for Monday morning; cafeteria will provide coffee makers, specific food items, etc. Needless to say, you must think through your needs in advance, so that you can run the meeting efficiently.

Think about your communication requirements on tournament day. Perhaps you want to be linked by cell phone or walkie-talkie to the persons in charge of the play competition, the cafeteria, and the tab room. That will enable you to talk with them if you are in route somewhere. Perhaps seeing that each location has a telephone is sufficient. It is important to attend to this communication detail at the outset.

Write memos to staff. I suggest three memos, the first a month or so in advance of the tournament, detailing plans to use their rooms, a second memo a few days before the tournament, and one on the first school day following the tournament. Following are examples:

MEMO 1

TO: CARL HAYDEN FACULTY & STAFF
FROM: T. Heathcotte, D. Fornatora, & Speech Team
SUBJ: AIA Speech & Theatre State Finals

On Friday and Saturday, April 2 and 3, the Carl Hayden Speech Team will host State Finals. The tournament will begin at 8:00 a.m. on Friday in the Auditorium. At 2:00 p.m. on Friday, debate rounds will begin in the 200 Building, the 1300 Building and Rooms 302 and 303. (Since this day is an end-of-the-semester grading day, I hope you teachers in these buildings won't mind.)

On Saturday, rooms in the 200, 300, 800, 1200, 1300 Buildings, the Library, and the Cafeteria will be in use. Computerized classrooms will not be used, but practically every other room will be. Please secure important materials, such as grade books, personal computers, calculators, etc. It is a good idea to lock your file cabinets and desks. We rarely have problems with vandalism or theft at tournaments, but it helps to remove temptation.

The tournament staff will make every effort to see that your rooms are left as we found them; however, I hope you will be understanding....as you always are....if things are a bit awry on Monday morning.

If you have any students who would like to help out for the experience of being at State Finals, please send them to one of us. We will need several student guides and runners. This is an excellent opportunity for you to get your students interested in an academic activity.

We invite you to attend the tournament to see some of the best talent in the State of Arizona competing in your very classrooms. Thank you for your continued help and support of the speech and drama program here at Hayden.

MEMO 2

TO: CARL HAYDEN FACULTY & STAFF
FROM: T. Heathcotte, D. Fornatora, & Speech Team
SUBJ: AIA Speech & Theatre State Finals
This is a reminder that State Finals will be held this weekend. If your room is going to be used, be sure to stash your stuff.

Thanks again for your help.

MEMO 3
TO: CARL HAYDEN FACULTY & STAFF
FROM: T. Heathcotte, D. Fornatora, & Speech Team
SUBJ: AIA Speech & Theatre State Finals

Thank you for your help and cooperation in making our tournament such a success. If there is any problem with your room today, please contact one of us. Thanks.

—the invitation packet

First, decide what schools you are going to invite. If your tournament is sponsored by your governing body, you'll probably be handed a list of schools to invite. However, if you are doing an invitational on your own, you can choose the schools you want. In any case, you can get the schools' addresses in your own activities office by asking for the interscholastic association book. The addresses will probably include the names of speech coaches, as well.

The invitation itself is a packet of information, which should include a letter of invitation with events offered, entry deadline, and costs. Include an entry form that delineates numbers of events offered, maximum student entries, judges' names, and a place for computing the costs of competition. If your governing body has a standard form, duplicate it and use it. If not, you might phone a speech coach in a neighboring school and find out what entry blank has been used recently at other tournaments and what prevailing costs are. Those costs will be higher if you plan to give trophies, since you must pay for the trophies out of your entry fees.

Other items you might want to put into the packet are: a map of your school with perhaps a list on the back of fast-food places close by; a schedule of the rounds; motel information for out-of-town teams; and a description of your stage and lighting design if a play competition is a part of the tournament.

If you intend to include the food and motel information, you need to call the restaurants in advance to alert them to the influx of students on tournament day. Restaurants that rely on serving school populations tend to cut back workers on Saturday. That could play havoc with your tournament time schedule. If McDonald's is very slow in serving your tournament entrants, you could find yourself delaying afternoon rounds. Also, it's important to contact the motels in advance for room availability. Some of them will extend special rates for tournament.

Following are some models for the invitation packet:

(Use your school letterhead)

Welcome Coaches and Competitors:

NAME OF TOURNAMENT
Date of Contest
Your High School

EVENTS: Interpretation of Serious Prose, Poetry, Drama, Humor, Duo Acting, Duo Interpretation, Original Oratory, Extemporaneous Speaking, Policy & L-D Debate

ENTRIES: Each school may enter five students in each category. A student may enter only two categories, except policy debaters who may enter only policy. All entries are due by Friday, November 30.
Drops may be phoned in until December 6.
Fees will be assessed at that time.
Phone: 602-271-2419 (after 11:00 a.m.)
Mail entries to Tournament Director at the address above.

FEES: Individual event entries are $3 each. Team entries are $6. Play fee is $20. Base fee is $15. Each coach must bring some form of payment at the time of registration..School checks or purchase orders, copies of school requisitions, personal checks, or cash will be accepted. Make checks payable to Carl Hayden Speech Team.

JUDGES: Each school must bring 1 judge for every 5 entries in individual and duo events, 1 judge for every 2 policy or L-D entries. Fractions over require another judge. A $20 fine may be assessed for lack of sufficient judges.

L-D TOPIC: Resolved, that government limits on the individual's right to bear arms in the United States is justified.

DEBATE QUARTER FINALS: Will be held if there are more than 32 entries in any event.

REGISTRATION: Friday from 3:30 to 4:00 p.m.
                        Saturday from 7:00 to 7:30 a.m.
                        Lobby of Auditorium
                        Park in 35th Avenue parking lot.

REMINDERS TO COACHES:
Copies of orations must be submitted at registration.
SCHOOLS MAY NOT ENTER UNLESS NFL DUES ARE PAID.
In interpretation events, no recorded material may be used unless it is also in print and copyrighted.
Ballots will rank competitors from 1 to 7. Bring stopwatches for all judges.
Remind judges that competitors have a right to call for time signals.
Breaking to finals is calculated on cumulative of the day.

FOOD: Snack food and soft drinks will be on sale on the campus throughout the tournament. There are many fast food restaurants within walking distance.

My speech team and I are looking forward to seeing you. If you have any questions, please feel free to call.

Sincerely yours,

Tournament Director

TOURNAMENT ENTRY FORM

SCHOOL_____
      COACH_____

PHONE_____
HOME PHONE_____

PLEASE RETURN THIS COMPLETED FORM TO YOUR TOURNAMENT DIRECTOR NO LATER THAN_____

Type (or print legibly) first and last names of each participant. Place an * by the names of those contestants who are entered in two events.

HUMOR———————————————————
SERIOUS PROSE—————————————
POETRY_____
DRAMA_____
ORATORY_____
EXTEMPORANOUS_____

LINCOLN-DOUGLAS DEBATE_____
POLICY DEBATE_____
DUO ACTING_____
DUO INTERPRETATION_____
(Leave room for six entries or however many your state
allows in each category

LIST JUDGES (indicate category)

PLAY COMPETITION
Title
Author
Names of students-cast & crew

ENTRY FEES
MAKE CHECK OR
NUMBER OF ENTRIES PER EVENT   FEES
PO PAYABLE TO:
HUMOR   ($3.00 per entry)   =
SERIOUS   "   "   =
AIA Tournament Director
POETRY   "   "   =
DRAMA   "   "   =
ORATORY   "   "   =
EXTEMP   "   "   =
L-D DEBATE   "   "   =
POLICY   "   "   =
DUO ACTING   ($6.00 per entry =
DUO INTERP   "   "   =
PLAY   ($20 per play)   =
BASE FEE   ($15 per school)   =
                      TOTAL

ROUNDS SCHEDULE / L-D & POLICY DEBATE

Friday, December 7:

3:30 PM	REGISTRATION (Auditorium Lobby
4:00 PM	ROUND I
DINNER BREAK	
6:30 PM	ROUND II
8:00 PM	ROUND III

Saturday, December 8:

12:00 N	QUARTER FINALS (If more than 32 teams)
1:30 PM	SEMI-FINALS
3:30 PM	FINALS
6:00 PM	AWARDS ASSEMBLY (Auditorium)

SCHEDULE OF INDIVIDUAL EVENTS ROUNDS

7:30 AM   REGISTRATION (Auditorium Lobby)
7:30 AM   EXTEMP DRAW I (Library)
7:45 AM COACHES AND JUDGES MEETING
(Auditorium)
8:00 AM   ROUND I
9:00 AM   EXTEMP DRAW II
9:30 AM   ROUND II
10:30 AM   EXTEMP DRAW III
11:00 AM   ROUND III
LUNCH BREAK
1:30 PM   COACHES' REVIEW
2:00 PM   SEMI-FINALS
4:00 PM   COACHES' REVIEW
4:30 PM   FINALS
6:00 PM   AWARDS ASSEMBLY (Auditorium)

—*making room assignments*

Before making any room assignments, get a map of the school or a list of available rooms from the assistant principal in charge of facilities. He or she may have already suggested that some rooms are not appropriate, such as computer labs or woodshops. Certainly, when you send your first memo to teachers, you'll hear from many of them that their rooms should not be used for a variety of reasons, including fear that their stapler will be stolen. But, many will have valid reasons for not using their rooms.

This will have to be a judgment call on your part. Sometimes you'll just have to say you're sorry but you have to use the rooms. A lot depends on the number of rooms available on your campus and how generally cooperative your staff tends to be. If some teachers are difficult, you may have to get the assistant principal to help you field complaints. For the most part, however, ninety percent of teachers are pretty cooperative.

Once you've got your room list in hand, actually walk the campus and look at the rooms to make certain they are suitable. You don't want the embarrassment of assigning an oratory round to a broom closet. Also, such blunders delay tournament day itself.

Now you're ready to assign rooms to events. Assign them by groups, such as all poetry rounds in one area or building. Put extemp close to the library and duo acting close to the auditorium. In addition, when you assign rooms for semi-final and final rounds, as much as possible use the same locations that you used for the preliminary rounds because competitors will know where to find the rooms.

An exception might be that you may want to condense the number of areas or buildings you are using by the end of the tournament, so that janitors might begin to clean and close up. In that case, you'll probably want to put your semi-final and final rounds in one area. Be sure to choose an area that has large classrooms, however, because competitors who do not make the out-rounds generally want to watch them, creating rather large audiences.

Once room assignments are made, type them up and print several copies. Pass copies of the assignments out to the tab room workers, maintenance workers, security, principals, or anyone else with an interest.

—ordering supplies

There are many supplies you'll need for your preliminary work and for tournament day. Be sure to have a large stock of duplicating paper, so you can make copies of ballots, entry blanks, rounds sheets, maps, etc. Additionally, you will need marking pens, posterboard for posting outrounds, envelopes for your invitations, rulers, staplers, white out, masking tape, paper clips, and any other office supplies currently in use.

A local grocery store will happily give you clean grocery sacks (easy advertising) for collecting the reams of judge's ballots. Set the sacks up with school codes marked on them.

You'll need a receipt book and a cashbox for registration. If you are planning to do food sales, you'll need cash boxes for those locations, as well.

You'll want to arrange in advance for whatever awards you are going to give. If awards must go to a printer, leave time for the printing. Order your trophies in advance also, so that they can be made up.

You'll probably want to make up some signs in advance that say things like "Registration this way" or Tab Room" with an arrow. Then on the day of the tournament, your students can hang them up all over campus, so your guests won't get lost. These signs can simply be handwritten on paper. Or, they can be elaborately designed using computer graphics.

At some tournaments your ballots will be prepared for you and handed to you. At other tournaments you will have to get the printing done yourself. Be certain how this works by checking with the president of your association.

Once the ballots are in your hands, you will want to set up a time, preferably with your team present to help, when you count and fold the ballots and put them into envelopes. Actually, this can be a fun little spirit builder. It helps them take ownership of hosting the tournament.

—feeding coaches, judges, and competitors

Food at a tournament is a full-time job for one person, so be sure you have another teacher to help you. Whoever does the work, these are the things that need to get done.

There are two kinds of food at a tournament—free/ hospitality food for coaches, judges, and tournament workers and the kind that is paid for by the consumer, mostly competitors. Both kinds have to be ordered, picked up, prepared, and cleaned up after. Be sure to plan for all those functions.

Hospitality food will vary, depending on the size of the tournament and the number of workers. It's important to remember that the food costs must come out of the entry fees along with trophies and other supplies. Plan the menus within your financial means, then be a smart shopper. Use discount stores and bulk savings stores. Buy as much as you can in advance of the day. Then someone can make quick runs to the grocery as needed on tournament day.

Your reputation as a tournament director may be more influenced by the food you serve than the quality of your overall management skill. People care about their stomachs; and, after all, tournament days are very long, so don't shirk on the quality of the food.

Serve quick, nourishing food and some general edibles (junk food). Then, cater the main meal(s) for people who have to remain at the tournament site all day, that is, the tab room workers, student workers in the play competition, and some judges.

Be sure to set out extra trashcans on campus.

Following is a sample of a plan for food:

    Rolling cart, tubs for soft drinks
    Call caterer
    Pick up doughnuts

Friday 7 a.m.
Green Room /17 aud workers & play judges
Doughnuts, bagels, cream cheese, orange juice, cups, napkins, cream, sugar, stirrers

Friday noon
Green Room / 17 aud workers and play judges
Catered Mexican food

Friday 2-9 p.m.
Green Room / 17 aud workers and play judges
Room 301 / 50 debate coaches & judges
15 tabbers & student volunteers
Soft drinks, pretzels, chips, salsa, paper plates, napkins, small candies

Friday 6 p.m.
Cafeteria / 150 debaters, coaches, & judges
Pizza by order—Jenny will make the run to Peter Piper

Saturday 7 a.m.
Green Room / 17 aud workers & play judges
Room 302 / 25 tabbers and workers

Cafeteria / 80 coaches and judges
Doughnuts, bagels, cream cheese, orange juice, cups, napkins, cream, sugar, stirrers

Saturday 2 p.m.
Green Room / 17 aud workers & play judges
Room 302 / 25 tabbers and workers
Catered Mexican food

Saturday 2-6 p.m.
Green Room / 17 aud workers and play judges
Cafeteria / 80 coaches & judges

Room 302 / 25 tabbers & student volunteers
Soft drinks, pretzels, cupcakes, paper plates, napkins

The other kind of food at a tournament is the kind your speech team can make some money on. They can set up and man...or woman...a candy stand throughout the entire tournament. They can vary what they sell with the time of day; that is, doughnuts, orange juice, and milk in the morning; soft drinks, candy bars, popcorn, chips later in the day. Competitors, judges, and coaches will all drop by and buy items.

The little enterprise is lucrative and simple. All it takes is a rolling cart, a moneybox, and a couple of students who are trustworthy. The adult you have in charge of the hospitality food can make a few grocery store runs to replenish supplies throughout the day, as needed.

You may decide to include other clubs and organizations in the food selling, particularly if your school is remote and/or no fast food places are close by. Under those circumstances, it may be to your advantage to involve the parent booster club and other clubs on campus. They could set up hot dog stands, Indian fry bread booths, or any other kind of food booth they wish in a food bazaar format. Should you choose this method, be sure to advertise it in your entry form. Also, be certain that other people take care of the details, not you.

—student volunteers

You will need student volunteers for many different jobs. Some of the jobs are: hall or building monitors, technical crew members for play competition, set up of signs, posting winners of semi-final and final rounds, tab room runners, ballot checkers, campus guides, and cleanup at the end of the tournament.

There are several methods for obtaining student volunteers. Certainly your own team members should participate. In fact, they will probably consider themselves hosts as well. Encourage that feeling in them. They may want to take on some of the task of finding student volunteers, if you ask them to do so.

Additionally, you can ask in your classes, perhaps giving them extra credit for participating. Ask other teachers in your department to do the same. Also, there are some kinship activities where you might find some willing volunteers, such as in student government, on the baseball team, and in JROTC. They often see it as their advantage to participate in prestigious events, such as a speech tournament.

Once you have a group of volunteer students, set up a schedule for them. Perhaps some will want to work all day; others only half day. With volunteers, one needs to be accommodating. Don't ask them to do more work or spend more time than they willingly volunteer for, or they won't show up at all. After you have made their assignments, give them something tangible to hold their commitments in their minds.

Following is a model you might use.

STATE FINALS VOLUNTEER:
Thank you for volunteering to help with Speech & Theatre State Finals. Here is your schedule. If there is a problem with it, please let me know so that I may reschedule. Thank you. Ms. Heathcotte

NAME:　　　Sam Goodfellow
DAY:　　　　Friday, April 2
TIME:　　　　4:00 p.m. to 6:00 p.m.
PLACE:　　　Student parking lot
ACTIVITY:　Campus guide for competitors

—tab room workers

For your tournament to run well, you're going to need some tab room workers who know what they are doing. If you know any seasoned coaches by now, call and ask them to work in your tab room. As the entry blanks begin to come in, you can see what schools will be attending. Choose some of them, particularly schools with big teams, and ask the coach to work in the tab room. Most tab rooms function best with about eight to ten coaches working.

Choose a coach you know and trust to function as your tab room director. Otherwise, you will be too confined during the actual tournament. You should remain free to move around...to go to the cafeteria to check on food supplies or unlock an extra classroom.

Ask the tab room director to name an ethics committee of three to five coaches who are working in the tab room. This is very important in the event there are any challenges to decisions made by judges or challenges regarding violations of tournament rules.

If you have chosen a good coach to oversee the tab room, you've got a pretty good chance of having a first class tournament. Give some thought to which person you'll ask.

The same is true if you are running a play competition. Make certain you have a coach or a drama teacher, perhaps the one from your own school, who will run the play competition according to the tournament rules. Also, the auditorium will be used exclusively for the play competition, so don't plan anything else there throughout the day.

Generally, you'll have shows going on all day long. You'll want to develop a schedule that allows a cast to put its set up in the scene shop, go into the dressing room, perform, and receive critique. Then, it's a simple matter to assign each succeeding play. As soon as the first cast goes into the dressing room, the next cast can line up its set, following in the order of the first cast. You can keep shows going this way all day long if you have a few drama students to oversee each area, that is, scene shop, dressing rooms, backstage, control booths.

Additionally, you need to have a coach in charge of the extemporaneous event. This event usually happens around the library because the competitors use the magazines and/or the tables to prepare their speeches for the judges. Make sure the coach who runs this event realizes he or she needs to develop some topics the students can talk about. If you are running an impromptu event in your tournament, you will need to do the same for it.

Be sure you have sets of the tournament rules avail-able in the tab room, in the library, and in the audito-rium.

—coding, setting rounds and assigning judges

These aspects of running a tournament are most often gov-erned by the rules of the governing body. **Be sure to fol-low the rules**, so that your tournament will be successful. Slipping up on rules in rounds setting or judge assignment can cause ethics committee problems and delays on tour-nament day, not to mention bad feelings on the parts of competitors, judges, and coaches. Following are some general procedures to augment your governing body's rules.

As entry blanks come in, be sure to assign a school code. That means to assign a letter of the alphabet to the school, then a number to each competitor. Thus, an inter-per in humor becomes S-14, while his teammate in L-D debate is S-27. With such a coding system, you can insure more fairness on the part of judges because they will not know the student's school or name and won't display prejudice for or against the student.

You should set up panels according to a set of rules that encompasses the following: Students don't compete against members of their own team or against the same people from other schools in more than one round. There are some formulas for setting rounds so that this won't happen. In fact, there are computer programs designed to set rounds. All you have to do is input the names and codes. It's probably worth a few phone calls to other coaches to see if you can turn up such a program and save yourself some hours of work, setting rounds.

Once you have set up the rounds appropriately, you can assign judges to them. Be sure to assign judges according to the categories attached to their name on the entry blank...as much as possible. Additionally, don't assign a judge to a panel where a student from his/her school is competing. Also, as much as possible, avoid assigning judges to evaluate the same competitors more than once. When you have set the rounds with judges, assign rooms according to the list you have already made.

You can assemble the whole list of panels for each event on one piece of paper. It should look something like this:

PAIRINGS FOR EXTEMP - ROUND I

Section 1 Room 802	Section 2 Room 803	Section 3 Room 804
S-11	BB-36	CC-5
B-9	E-36	B-12
G-5	T-12	S-37
Y-14	JJ-3	JJ-4
JJ-1	CC-6	N-17
E-32	B-10	E-33
Judge:	Judge	Judge:
CC-Fong	Y-Smith	D-Rawls

After these rounds are developed for each event, copies should be made for each school and put in the registration packets. Or, post the pairings in several locations on campus. That saves a few trees.

One note about obtaining judges: Your governing body may require each coach to provide a certain number of judges per entrants or per team. If this is not the case, you will need to obtain your own judges. They can come from your own alumni, your speech team parents, other teachers, or community people, such as lawyers, business people, or actors. Also, if there is a junior college or university nearby, you could call a speech professor and ask for some college students to judge. It's good to have a few extra judges on hand just in case you have need of them on tournament day.

—*tournament day*

In advance of tournament day, prepare packets for each school. In a large envelope, place a copy of the school's tournament entry, several maps of the school, several schedules of rounds, a list of instructions to judges if one is a part of your rules book, the ballots for each judge, and a list of fast food restaurants. Note: Some tournament hosts prefer to issue ballots individually to judges rather than putting them in the packets. The rationale here is that the tab room can keep closer control over what judge is used. Here again, just do whatever is the prevailing method for your first tournament.

Set up a table in some place convenient to your school's parking lot. Place three or four adults behind the table to receive money and purchase orders for entries. It's also very important to have someone here to write down drops from the tournament.

High school students being what they are, often times a coach will arrive minus some of the competitors listed on the entry form.

After registration, the list of drops should be delivered in a timely fashion to the coaches in the tab room. With a quick check they can tell whether or not the drops will mean a panel might be harmed. For example, if a panel falls below 4 competitors, the people in the tab room may want to shift those competitors to another panel. If that happens, you can put a note on the door of the classrooms involved or you might just say so in your opening assemby. Most of the time this doesn't happen, but it's important to watch for, just in case there is a decimated panel.

Opening assemblies are sometimes appropriate. You need to decide if you want one. Things you might need to talk about are: judging rules, modified panels because of drops, tournament rule changes, reminders to be clean and tidy and polite.

Once the first round starts, magic happens. You've set it all in motion with your lists and phone calls. Everyone knows what to do, and they just do it, following the schedule you created.

As tournament director it is important for you to move around, make certain things are progressing as they should, put out fires when they arise, and display a general presence at the tournament. As the day unfolds, you will feel a happy hum inside, knowing you have planned competently and appropriately and that all is going as projected.

If you have arranged for a copying machine so that the tab room workers can make copies of all their tab sheets to put into the packets for each school, the end of the tournament will run smoothly. All of the competitors should receive their critique sheets from their judges. This is where the grocery sacks come into play. Collect those grocery sacks and stack them along the front of the stage at the awards assembly.

At the end of the day, the awards assembly will give closure to the whole event. Take some care to see that all of the important workers at your tournament receive credit, that the trophies are displayed prominently, and that you know who won what events. Take your bow graciously, too. It's hard work to direct a tournament.

—after the tournament

Besides the staff memo of thanks, send thank you notes to all of your student volunteers, the coaches who worked tab, the maintenance, security, and clerical staff members who did extra duty for the tournament, and to all the people you can think of who went out of their way for you.

Write a press release telling who the winners were in each category. Send it to the local newspaper and to your own school newspaper.

Indulge in a holiday weekend with your significant other!

CHAPTER 7

Teaching in the Inner City

Not all of the new speech and drama teachers who read this book will be employed in an inner city school, but a great many will be. This chapter is a personal perspective from me to the ones who do.

When I began teaching in the inner city, my heart was full of a desire to do some good, to make the inner city a better place, and especially to have a positive impact on my students. I thought I could turn their lives around and head them into a fulfilling future. I know that I have been successful with some students. Perhaps you have some goals like that, too. They were good goals then, and they're good goals now. I hope some of these ideas help you achieve yours.

All over the United States, high schools are becoming more inner city, more financially disadvantaged, more multi-cultural. The challenge for high school speech and theatre educators is to respond to the changing faces of their students and do so in a way that maintains the program quality while responding to the needs of student participants.

Preserving the heritage of O'Neill, Wilder, Shakespeare, and Shaw, though a worthy goal, is not enough. The challenges are more difficult...to incorporate the richness of Hispanic, Oriental, and Afro-American culture into the study of speech and drama and to teach standards of artistic expression that can be universally accepted.

—qualities I've noticed in inner city students

In many ways there aren't any differences between inner city students and students in any other schools. They all care very much about their clothes, about their hair, and about what each other thinks. Many of them want to go to school and prepare for a future. They fall in love too hard and hurt a great deal. They struggle to understand themselves and to figure out who they are in the world.

There are, however, some differences in the lives and behavior of inner city students that are important to know. By virtue of the fact that they live in an urban, inner city area, they are more often exposed to violence and crime than are other students. They see and hear more gunshots. They witness or are victims of more thefts. They drop out of school more often for a great variety of reasons that often include having to get a job to help support other family members, getting pregnant and/or married, and running away from home. They also drop out of school because they find it boring, confining, and a waste of time.

Those who remain in school are often hyperactive, unable to concentrate for very long, and very quick to give up on tasks. **It's important for the teacher to create a strong structure so the students will clearly understand the projected outcome of any tasks and all of the steps along the way to get there.**

Some examples: if you want to teach the students theatre terminology, you will have more success creating a game that requires them to say "scene shop," "stage right," or "blocking" than you will have if you ask them to write out the definitions of these words. If you want students to show respect for their judges at tournament, you must tell them what respect "looks like" and what it "sounds like."

It's incorrect to say that inner city students are less mature than other students; however, their behavior may lead one to that conclusion, particularly because of their propensities to talk a lot and move around aimlessly. I think, in fact, that it's not maturity that's the problem; it's the difficulty with focusing attention for very long. Often inner city students are more mature than others because of stressful life situations they have been forced to encounter at early ages. They are "street smart" more often than "school smart."

As an example, I once had an actress who had been very dependable in one show and had been on my speech team for several months doing quite well. She began missing rehearsals with lame excuses. When I finally told her I didn't believe her excuses, she got angry and walked away; but, an hour later she began to cry. She confided to me that she was afraid to come to rehearsal because her father had been binging on drugs and beating up on her mother. The student said he didn't do it when she and her brother were there, so she ditched rehearsals.

What appeared to be immature behavior (missing rehearsals and lying) **was in fact a display of mature emotion**, that of wanting to protect her mother. The student showed even more maturity by accepting my suggestion of a protective service where her mother could go and some courage in seeing that her mother got there.

Another characteristic of inner city students is particularly important to speech and drama teachers. That is their lack of artistic experiences. Not only have they seldom had any lessons in the arts, such as a dance class or music lessons, they have seldom even been to see a play in a theatre. Their knowledge of forensic activities, even the meaning of the word, is negligible. They will not have had a video camera in their home. They will probably never have heard their voice on tape or seen their image on television.

Be prepared to teach from the ground up. Take them to see shows; record speeches and interpretations for them to see on video. Use articulation practices. Videotape practices and rehearsals and use them as an aid to critique. Teach them how good audiences behave. Expect to begin at the beginning.

—some thoughts on fear and violence at school

Another observation I've made about inner city students is that they frequently won't make eye contact with a teacher when they see the teacher out on campus or in the nity, even though they may like the teacher very much. The reason for this behavior is that they are afraid that, if they do speak, they'll be ridiculed by their peers. For many young people, the teacher is a much safer person to ignore than a friend, if you could call such an intimidating associate "friend."

There is a lot of fear in the inner city. It's not just all on the streets, either. Remember that old saw that "the whole child comes to school"? Well, it's never been more true than it is today. **Many young people are afraid in their homes, in their neighborhoods, and on their school campuses.**

What that translates to at school is a student who is only partially focused on his or her future, like a goal to become a florist or an airplane mechanic. The other part of the young person's awareness is focused on staying whole...literally in one physical piece....on not becoming a random object of violence. Sometimes fear drives young people into real craziness like asking to be "jumped" into a gang. (That means being willing to run through a lineup of gang members, letting them beat you, if you're a guy. Or, allowing the male gang members to have sex with you, if you're a girl.) These are bizarre methods of keeping oneself "safe."

The most intimidating aspect of violence is its randomness. If you know you're inviting a physical attack by an insult or an angry response, that's one kind of violence, the kind one can prepare for, at least to some extent. The other kind of violence comes out of the blue: a bullet through the bedroom window while one is sleeping or a fist in the face for smiling hello to one's speech teacher.

On a personal level, it's important for you to know how to avoid setting yourself up for attack, either verbally or physically. Even though there are generally stringent punishments for students who attack teachers physically, the best thing for you (and your nose) is to avoid the situation. Verbal attacks are more difficult to avoid, but here are a few helpful techniques.

When students are angry with you, don't confront them with your own anger, even though you might feel it yourself. Remind yourself that their anger is misplaced. They are taking their hostility out on you, but you are not the primary cause of it. Remember that they have very little control over their anger. You have more.

In an angry confrontation, remain calm: especially keep a calm voice. Decide what the best course of action should be, i.e., to call security, to send the student out alone, to send another student for help. Then, once you've decided, insist on it. Keep playing "broken record" until the angry student backs down or help comes. For example, keep saying "I want you to take this pass and go to the activities office." Repeat it twenty times if you have to. Once the student is gone, you can decide what a more definite solution might be.

In the matter of disciplinary referral, I suggest that fewer is better. If you write many referrals, you'll begin to get a bad reputation in the front office as a teacher who can't control students. Resolve all conflicts within your area as much as possible. Then, when a student genuinely is out of control, the administrator in charge of discipline will usually be very willing to help you.

The teacher in the inner city school cannot solve all of the problems of students, no matter how much he or she might wish to do so.

But, knowing the problems exist is freeing for the teacher psychologically. Knowing allows the teacher to invent new frames of reference in class. It allows coaches and directors to create free space within their own time with their students, where true trust is born. Sharing and positive outcomes for the students can emerge from such a framework.

My advice here is to be alert to what you can do to help and offer assistance when you feel it's appropriate or when you feel you have an answer that might work. Try to make yourself easy to talk to so your students become willing to tell you their problems.

On the other hand, don't worry or get upset if you don't have an answer. Being their teacher, director, or coach is what you were hired to do. It is also, by the way, what the students expect of you. No one person is going to solve the problems of the inner city. Sorry...not even you!

But, if you work there, you can go home at night feeling very good about yourself when you've tried to understand your students and teach them, in spite of all the strikes they seem to have against them. Learn to look for small signs of progress, maybe a smile from a troubled student instead of a constant frown. Or, a growing willingness to come to practice. Once in a while you'll get a miracle: some of them not only survive but overcome, develop their talents and skills, and become lawyers, sales managers, and movie stars.

—goal setting and realization

Goal setting is unrealistic among many inner city students. It is often either too grandiose or too meager. For example, a student may have a goal in life to be a doctor but be unwilling to take any science classes in school. Or, on the other hand, a student may have considerable singing talent and yet plan on becoming a cosmetologist. Not that there's anything wrong with being a cosmetologist; it's just that such a career ignores a special singing talent that might bring a successful career with much money and personal satisfaction. The point is that students sometimes fail to recognize and capitalize on their viable talents and skills.

Not only do inner city students often need help with adjusting their career goal sights, they also can use assistance with thinking through the steps in between. For example, a student on your speech team might have a goal to become a lawyer but fear debate. It will be up to you to convince the student that debating is a definitive step toward his or her career goal. Scouting colleges while you're out on the tournament circuit is something you'll want to discuss with the student and then see that it happens. **You, as the teacher, will probably have to take a more decisive hand in opening your students' minds to the possibilities and ramifications of their goals.**

Such unrealistic goal setting and follow through arise out of a more general tendency to inhibition in creative and academic risk taking. At bottom there is a sense of self-doubt that is probably normal for all teens. But, in the inner city students tend to have low self-esteem and poor self-images. All they have to do is watch television to see that their homes and their neighborhoods are not desirable. Commercials especially encourage desires to have material goods and services that are not readily affordable in the average inner city home.

Neighborhoods, such as the ones they live in, are portrayed as bad places on television, as places to be avoided and protected from. Students in the inner city are as intelligent as any other human beings, and they realize they are on the bottom of the financial, if not the social, rung of society's ladder. Therefore, they often have low self-esteem, which causes them to hesitate to risk in many situations, including both academically and creatively.

Sometimes their fear of failure is so strong that they are unwilling even to try. This is noticeable in class rooms where they will not try to do an assignment rather than risk failing. In practices or rehearsal they often fear failing artistically. For example, if you as a director ask them to try to create a gesture for a character, they may refuse to use any gestures at all, holding their hands to their sides and looking down. You may find you have to give them a gesture, even model it for them. They need assurances and encouragement from you to overcome their fear of failure and their societal conditioning to fail.

—teacher approaches and expectations

Assuming these qualities, characteristics, and attitudes that I've spoken about exhibit themselves in your school, I suggest the following approaches and expectations will help you keep your programs viable. Overall, keep in mind that the way you do school in the inner city is different from the way you do it in more affluent communities.

Look for modern pieces, i.e., play scripts, poetry, short stories that have been written in the last few years, particularly by non-white writers. Perhaps you can find some original works done by a local arts project. Your students may be able to relate to these materials more readily than to more classical or traditional materials.

Remain flexible with emergencies or accepting of reasons, i.e., "I can't come to rehearsal because I have to baby-sit" or "The truck broke down on my way to catch the van." Actually, most of the excuses your students give you will be true. The problem arises in that you, as an individual, are subjected to far more excuses than you feel you can endure and still keep your program together. For your own sanity, keep your expectations within the realm of reality.

Recast more as you go through a rehearsal schedule rather than continue to nag a student who is not going to come through. Just accept that you'll probably have to recast some parts because of non-attendance. That's an added bite of time out of your schedule to bring the new actor up to rehearsal level. Just consider it a part of the job description.

Also, **be prepared to take a role yourself** in case of an emergency, that is, if a performer fails to make a curtain. I don't know of a single drama teacher who has not had to play at least one part in his or her career. It goes with the territory.

A positive note here is that you can expect that your actors will help you with this process. You can turn it into a learning experience by reminding the students of the importance of honoring commitments to the whole group. Also, your students can get an opportunity to experience what it's like to teach by taking on the responsibility of teaching the new actor or you to do the role.

Similarly all of these ideas apply as group dynamics for debate teams, duo interpretation, or other team forensics events. In all honesty, however, speech team members are less dependent on each other than play casts. As a result, it is possible to expect to hold a speech team together in spite of some members' not being able to compete. You may find your team remains smaller than teams from more affluent schools; however, you have every right to expect your team to be competitive. And, at least you won't have to face performing in one of your student's places.

It's not wise to assume that your students will know how to behave at rehearsal on their own campus or at another school during a tournament. You must detail your expectations for behavior, not once but many times. Take the way they behave around you as a cue. If they don't say "please" and "thank you" to you, you must remind them to do so for their judges at tournament. Tell them you expect them to let you know in advance if they can't attend a tournament. If you expect all actors to remain until the end of the rehearsal, you have to tell them...more than once, probably.

You must also detail expectations for specific tasks, i.e., student director, crew head, or team captain. Get into the habit of having a private conference with each student on whom you confer responsibility. Tell each of them in a direct, detailed manner what you expect. A good technique is to brainstorm the list of duties with the student. For example, a team captain must send in the entry blanks, plan lunch on the road, and call all team members at 5:00 a.m. on tournament day.

Once you have detailed all the expectations for the particular job, you need to supervise carefully. Ask questions, such as, "Have you sent in the entry blank yet?" or make timely statements, such as, 'Friday is the deadline for sending in the entry blank."

Here is an important perspective for you: **The performances and competitions themselves are less important than taking your students successfully through the processes required to get the show or the events ready.** For example, being required to show up for three coaching sessions before they are allowed to go to tournament creates a mindset in your students about the value of preparedness. In the process they might learn that being on time helps. Hopefully, they'll also start getting better at their tournament pieces and become more viable in tournament.

The same is true with a show. Just getting from the auditions to the performance will be a major accomplishment for some students. They will have a right to be very proud of sticking to the task of getting through a rehearsal schedule. It may be the first time in their lives that they honored such a long-term commitment.

Teaching commitment and responsibility to a group is critically important to the lives of your students and to society as a whole. Be proud of yourself for these successes. But, don't beat yourself up over failures. You can't take them too seriously or you'll frustrate yourself and become less effective.

—quick tips for production

- Rehearse a few small pieces until they are smooth before you go to performance.
- Ask alumni to help with sets and work with students.
- Assign short sections of lines to memorize, i.e., three pages per rehearsal.
- Run lines before rehearsal.
- Do character or period research as a cast project.
- Discuss set design, play themes, and character analysis with the whole cast.
- Have several reading rehearsals at the beginning to make certain students understand the show. Lines or references may not be a part of their experience, but they may not know they don't understand. For example, if they've only seen a digital clock, the phrase "a quarter after two" won't mean much. Sometimes lines are funny to you but aren't funny to students. Take time to explain the humor.

- Don't be discouraged if audiences are small. Even parents may not attend their children's performances. There may also be apathy on the part of the administration, faculty, and student body. Those are common situations in the inner city. It's important that you and your cast don't take meager attendance personally.
- Try some variety in your performances of main stage shows, for example:
  Perform on weeknights instead of weekends
  Send invitations to family and friends
  Limit or eliminate performances for whole student body if heckling becomes a problem.
  Try some alternatives to main stage shows:
  > Feature films and documentaries
  > Videotape productions
  > Elementary and junior high school tours
  > Theatre sports
  > Roving mime troupes

—*some thoughts on racial attitudes*

Black and Hispanic students often don't try out for plays or the speech team because they perceive those as "white activities." Minority students often do not view performing arts as meaningful or worthwhile, even if you've carefully chosen a show with meaty Hispanic or black roles, such as *Tender Lies* by Pahl Gilsenan, or *My Children, My Africa* by Athol Fugard. With film and television so much a part of their lives, potential performers may even know your casting requirements. Maddening as it is, many still won't come to auditions.

Finian's Rainbow portrays the lunacy of racism in a comical way, so I felt it would be a good vehicle for my community. It was one of the few shows I felt should be cast as close to racial lines as possible, although I did cast a Hispanic leprechaun. At auditions I filled all the parts except the black girl who sings Necessity. After rehearsals began, the cast and I tried to talk several black girls into taking the part. When we failed, an Italian-American girl volunteered. With stage makeup darker than her skin tone, she performed so convincingly that many in the audience believed my actress was a new black student.

Occasionally, you get a black or Hispanic student who is very committed to your program. When you do, you know you've got a person with courage because he or she is capable of bucking a considerable amount of peer pressure. Honor that student and prepare to support him or her emotionally. When performance time comes, the result could be good, bad, or awful. The student's friends might show up with flowers in hand or they might heckle throughout the performance until you or the security guards throw them out.

—*plays that have worked with inter-racial casting*

Here are some examples of plays you might use for different production goals. The list is by no means exhaustive. You might also consult the International Thespian Society's list of commonly produced high school shows.

Samuel French, Inc. prints a similar list in their

catalog. Also, Dramatic Publishing Company uses a lot of photography in their catalog, which can give you ideas for appropriate casting with several races.

With **old-time comedy pieces and melodramas**, you don't have to think about skin color. Cast for talent alone. It's all for fun anyway.

> *Arsenic and Old Lace* by Joseph Kesselring
> *Curious Savage* by John Patrick
> *The Death and Life of Sneaky Fitch* by James L.
>   Rosenberg
> *Dirty Work at the Crossroads* by Bill Johnson
> *Harvey* by Mary Chase
> *My Three Angels* by Sam and Bella Spewack
> *You Can't Take It With You* by Hart and Kaufman

Family-centered shows can have casting that conforms to one race within the family. Roles of characters outside the family can be cast from other races. Some liberties can be taken within the families, also, such as casting a white mother and an Hispanic son. You might have to edit your script somewhat, like writing in such lines as "my mother Sarah" or "Son, will you do so and so." Then the audience can keep the relationships straight when skin colors don't match. Some judgments need to be made about your community and its acceptance level.

> *Ordinary People* by Judith Guest, dramatized by
>   Nancy Gilsenan
> *And They Dance Real Slow in Jackson* by Jim
>   Leonard, Jr.

Inter-racial casting can add **metaphorical meaning** to shows with a strong symbolic component. This approach would include much of children's theatre where there are wonderful roles that any race could be cast in.

Alice in Wonderland (any author)
The Cave by Tim Kelly
The Crucible by Arthur Miller
The Interview by Jean-Claude van Itallie
J. B. by Archibald MacLeish

There are many good plays about **teen problems** or plays in which the primary roles are teens.

Addict or *Jury* by Jerome Mcdonough
Love, Death, and the Prom by John Jory
A Piece of My Heart by Shirley Lauro
Runaways by Elizabeth Swados
Voices from the High School by Peter Dee

Plays written around the **theme of prejudice** of any kind can be cast inter-racially to make strong statements.

Dark of the Moon by Howard Richardson and
        William Berney
The Doll's House by Henrik Ibsen
Flowers for Algernon by Daniel Keyes, dramatize
        by David Rogers
Inherit the Wind by Jerome Lawrence and
        Robert E. Lee
To Kill a Mockingbird by Harper Lee, dramatized
        by Christopher Sergel

Some plays lend themselves to **readers theatre** performance style and come off well with inter-racial casting, such as:

> *I Never Saw Another Butterfly* by Celeste
> Raspanti
> Spoon River Anthology by Charles Aidman,
> conceived from Edgar Lee Masters.

--rewards of inner city teaching

Recent polls have shown consistently that teaching high school in the inner city is one of the highest stress jobs there is. It ranks right up there with air traffic control, emergency room medicine, and police work. Make no mistake—it's more difficult to teach in the inner city than in more affluent communities.

No wonder that this is so. Theft is corrosive...so common that it is accepted as a part of life. Hostility toward teachers is epidemic. Young people are harassed on their school campuses. Many carry guns to school, believing they need them for protection. Cutting funds for education is a favorite pastime of legislatures. Teachers are overworked and under-supported. And, with each passing year, more social pressure is placed on them to parent their students and play the role of social worker. All of that is in addition to improving test scores, of course.

In both the classroom and the extra-curricular environment, teachers have to stretch to solve day-to-day problems with and for their students. Nothing is constant or predictable. You have to reevaluate, restructure, reinvent, reassess all the time.

So why is this segment headed "rewards of inner city teaching"? When it all works, you get a rush of love, pride, and accomplishment that is hard to beat anywhere because you know how very much it took to achieve the win. Imagine a student's face light up when he or she is named as a finalist in a speech tournament for the very first time. Now, that's a smile that lives in memory.

One of my speech team members was from an extremely poor household.   The family, consisting of four children and a mother, was on welfare, and the mother was terminally ill. When my student took first place in her event at a tournament, the family was so proud that they saved lunch money to buy her a new dress. She wore the new dress happily and won the next tournament as well. Her fellow team members and this coach were pretty proud and happy, too.

That pride and happiness turned to joy many times for me over the years and kept me willingly teaching in the inner city.   For me, it has truly been a path with a heart. It may be that for you, too. If so, God is blessing you as He has blessed me.

— *a theatre story*

Once not long ago I directed a show with a cast of twenty-five and a crew of five...typical in many ways of other casts I've had over the years but special because of their individuality. Following are some of their stories on the closing night of the show:

Kelly, a black male, the curtain puller, had cuts and bruises all over his face from a fight with his mother.

Martha, a Hispanic girl, had cuts on her wrists from an attempted suicide because her boyfriend was sent to jail.

Jack, a white male, lived with friends because his parents didn't want him. He drank a lot and brought me a rose before the performance.

Sally, a white girl, wore high-heeled boots, a mini skirt, and a chain belt. Her mother was a stripper in the nudie bar close to the school. Sally had miscarried a child earlier in the week and hoped to go to college and major in computers.

Natalia, a black girl, very overweight, smelled of marijuana cigarettes. Her father hated her because she looked like her dead mother.

Johnny, the Hispanic leading man, was in a car wreck on the way to the performance and had tiny slivers of glass up and down his arm, causing it to swell and turn red.

Rochelle, the Hispanic leading lady, seemed afraid all of the time. She couldn't understand why her mother wouldn't come to see her performances and was always angry with her.

Jeff, a white male, had his motorcycle stolen out of the parking lot during a rehearsal. No insurance.

Gloria, a Hispanic girl, cried because her father had died several months ago and could not come to see her performance.

Together these young people put aside the ugliness of their lives and, for two brief hours, acted in concert to create a beautiful illusion for the audience. They did all of the things I had told them to do in rehearsal...speak loudly and clearly, change the set, cover for another actor on a forgotten line, pull the curtain, cry on cue, kiss on cue. They suspended all of their life problems and acted as a single unit to bring pleasure to the audience.

Momentarily they lived in a world where theatre matters...where the loveliest ideas are expressed metaphorically...in the between-time of sound, color, light, and nuance. **All of the fine qualities of civilized society came together in the illusion of theatre these inner city students created.**

The school principals were not in attendance. Most of the members of the student body, the faculty, and many of their own parents were not there, either. But, the audience that was present was lucky...to enjoy the tender product of so much painful experience garnered from sixteen years of earthly life.

After the performance, the cast and crew gave me flowers. In their innocence they believed I had done something for them. And maybe I did. I gave them hope...in the importance of their work together...in the promise of some future...in the value of good articulation.

So much more they gave me. I sleep well at night, knowing the future is in their gentle, loving hands.

Resources

If you've gotten to this point in reading the book, you may feel somewhat overwhelmed by the time and energy required of a speech and/or drama teacher in a modern high school. Trust me, I know just how you feel. This is a demanding job you've undertaken. The concerns and stresses are major. It's important for you to have an awareness of that fact and plan accordingly. In other words, **take care of yourself.**

Stress in teaching comes from many places...the students, bells ringing, administrators, parents, your own standards. Add to that the "curtain-going-up" nature of speech and drama activities with the desire to create quality artistic products, and you've got a pressure cooker of a job. Here are some tips for taking care of yourself in both attitude and practice.

Make sure teaching is **a path with a heart** for you. Do you love teaching? Do you sincerely believe you can and want to make a difference in students' lives? If you have those beliefs, it might get rocky sometimes, but you'll survive.

Get into some kind of a support group with other teachers, friends, or family. If you can't find one, start one. There are lots of other teachers who want such a group. All teachers need to debrief in a safe environment. Then, be faithful to your group. Go to every meeting. Plan your team practices and rehearsal schedules so that you can. It's important for you to have a time to talk about your frustrations, your angers, your sadnesses. If you don't talk about them, you'll get weird or quit teaching. So, talk about them. **Be kind to yourself.**

You are likely to run across some negativity in school, on the part of some students or other school personnel. Remember, it takes energy to deal with negativity. If your personal life is going well, you can probably handle it. If there is some problem in your personal life, like the end of a love affair or a death in the family, you are less likely to be able to fend off the negativity at school. It's times like that when you will be most appreciative of a support group, if you have one.

There are down days—and down years—in teaching. Sometimes one class can be a downer, even though the other classes are fine. Dreading one hour out of your day for an entire school year is not pleasant.

Teacher burnout is a pernicious problem in the public schools. The teachers who care the most and want to do the best burn out. When they do, their effectiveness is dramatically diminished. Only you can keep yourself from becoming a statistic. A little knowledge about burnout can help you avoid it.

Burnout is happening when you feel overwhelmed by your job, when you have no personal life, when you can't say no, when you feel isolated from your peers, when you feel sad, angry, or depressed a lot, when you make a lot of small mistakes, when you feel over-involved but can't withdraw.

If you read these warning signs in yourself, take action quickly. Get into a support group, if you haven't already; read some self-help books; reduce your workload; cultivate a new interest outside school; take time off from school if necessary. It's important for you to rejuvenate yourself...find a new inspiration...**nurture and heal yourself.**

Then, you can return to your students with renewed vitality. Speech and drama are powerful vehicles because they allow students to explore their inner natures, to grow and realize much of their potential. It takes a whole, healthy teacher to stay with that kind of growth. You owe it to your students and to yourself to do what is needful in your own nurturance and care...to be the best you can be so that your students can be the best they can become.

BREAK A LEG!

Materials Catalogs

Baker's Plays
P. O. Box 699222
Quincy, MA 02269-9222
www.bakersplays.com/

Classroom Collection
Calloway House, Inc.
451 Richardson Drive
Lancaster, PA 17603-4098
www.callowayhouse.com/home.asp

Dramatic Publishing Company
311 Washington Street
P. O. Box 129
Woodstock, IL 60098
815-338-7170
Lots of good, rewritten novels and classics.

Dramatists Play Service, Inc.
440 Park Avenue South
New York, NY 10016
www.dramatists.com/
A major play publishing house

Eldridge Plays and Musicals
P. O. Box 1595
Venice, FL 34284
www.95church.com/
Christian Drama

Films for the Humanities & Sciences
P. O. Box 2053
Princeton, NJ 085432053
www.films.com

Greenhaven Press, Inc.
P. O. Box 289009
San Diego, CA 921987
www.galegroup.com/greenhaven/
Ask for Opposing Viewpoints Library/ Classroom Catalog

Language Arts Catalog
Perfection Learning Corporation
1000 North Second Avenue
Logan, Iowa 51546-1099
www.plconline.com

Music Theatre International
37 Edison Avenue
West Babylon, NY 11704-1008
631-491-0670

Pioneer Drama Service
P. O. Box 4267
Englewood, CO 80155-4267
www.pioneerdrama.com/

Samuel French, Inc.
45 West 25th Street
New York, NY 10010
www.samuelfrench.com/
Comprehensive catalog of plays and books about theatre arts. Their frequently produced shows list is helpful.

Spectrum Educational Media, Inc.
P. O. Box 611
Mattoon, IL 61938
www.spectrummedia-boston.com/

Tams-Witmark Music Library, Inc.
560 Lexington Avenue F-112
New York, NY 10022
212-688-2525

Wetmore Declamation Bureau
Box 2595
Sioux City, Iowa 51106-0595
712-276-3041

Theatrical Vendors

Costume Holiday House
3038 Hayes Avenue
Fremont, OH 43420
419-334-3236

Encore Theatrical Supply
5556 C Springdale Avenue
Pleasanton, CA 94588
www.globaldomain.com/encore/makeup.htm

The Great American Market
826 N. Cole Avenue
Hollywood, CA 90038
Gobos and gear
www.gamonline.com

Norcosto
500 N. Michigan Ave. Suite 1920
Chicago, IL 60611-3703
www.norcostco.com
Hardware, color media, costumes, makeup

PNTA Stage & Studio Supplies
333 Westlake Avenue North
Seattle, WA 98109
www.pnta.com

Rosco Laboratories, Inc.
36 Bush Avenue
Port Chester, NY 10573
Color media, special effects
www.rosco.com

SECOA
8650 109th Ave. N
Champlin, MN 55316-5519
www.secoa.com
Lights, sound, drapery, platforms, consumables

Theatre, Drama & Speech Resources
Contemporary Drama Service
805 Elkton Drive
Colorado Springs, CO 80907
719-594-4422

Ticket Craft
1390 Jerusalem Ave.
Merrick, NY 11566
516-538-6200

Useful One-Act Play Collections

No ratings provided. Consider the cultural climate where you teach. What works in one school won't in another. What works for speech competition might not work in night performance. You're the final judge of propriety.

10 Minute Plays:Actors Theatre of Louisville, Vol. 4 edited by Michael Bigelow Dixon and Liz Engelman, Samuel French: New York, 1998.

20 One-Act Plays from 20 Years of the Humana Festival edited by Michele Volanski and Michael Bigelow Dixon, Smith & Kraus: Lyme, NH, 1995.

24 Favorite One-Act Plays edited by Bennet Cerf and Van H. Cartmell, Dolphin Books: New York, 1963.

15 American One-Act Plays edited by Paul Kozelka, Pocket Books: New York, 1961.

The Ground Zero Club and Other Prize-Winning Plays edited by Wendy Lamb, Dell Publishing Company: New York, 1985.

Meeting the Winter Bike Rider and Other Prize-Winning Plays by Wendy Lamb, Dell Publishing Company: New York, 1985.

The Mentor Book of Short Plays edited by Richard H. Goldstone and Abraham H. Lass, New American Library: New York, 1969.

One-Act Plays for Acting Students edited by Norman A. Bert, Meriwether Publishing Company: Colorado Springs, CO, 1987.

Play It Again! More One-Act Plays for Acting Students edited by Norman A. Bert, Meriwether Publishing Company, Colorado Springs, CO, 1993.

Short Plays for Young Actors edited by Craig Slaight and Jack Sharrar, New Hampshire: Smith and Krauss, 1996.

Take Ten: New 10-Minute Plays edited by Eric Lane and Nina Shengold, Random House: New York, 1997.

Monologue and Scene Books

No ratings provided. Consider the cultural climate where you teach. What works in one school won't in another. What works for speech competition might not work in night performance. You're the final judge of propriety.

50 Great Scenes for Student Actors edited by Lewy Olfson, Bantam Books: New York, 1980.

57 Original Auditions for Actors by Eddie Lawrence, Meriwether Publishing Ltd.: Colorado Springs, 1988.

The Actor's Book of Monologues for Women collected by Stefan Rudnicki, Penguin Books: New York, 1991.

The Actor's Scenebook edited by Michael Schulman and Eva Mekler, Bantam Books: New York, 1984.

The Actor's Scene Book, Volume II edited by Michael Schulman and Eva Mekler, Bantam Books: New York, 1987.

Audition Monologues for Student Actors edited by Roger Ellis, Meriwether Publishing Company: Colorado Springs, CO, 1999.

Contemporary American Monologues for Women edited by Todd London, Theatre Communication Group: New York, 1998.

Extreme Exposure: An Anthology of Solo Performance Texts from the Twentieth Century edited by Jo Bonney, Theatre Communication Group: New York, 2000.

Film Scenes for Actors edited by Joshua Karton, Bantam Books: New York, 1983.

Film Scenes for Actors Volume II edited by Joshua Karton, Bantam Books: New York, 1987.

Modern Scenes for Student Actors edited by Wynn Handman, Bantam Books: New York, 1978.

Scenes for Student Actors (six volumes) edited by Frances Cosgrove, Samuel French, Inc.: New York, 1958.

Solo: The Best Monologues of the 80's edited by Michael Earley and Phillippa Keil, Applause Books, New York, 1987.

Professional Associations

—teaching

There are two major professional organizations for teachers, both of which have state and local affiliates. You will probably be asked by teachers in your school to join one or both of them. It is important for you to belong to one organization or the other for two reasons. One is the professional affiliation with other teachers for political power to improve teaching conditions, salary/benefits, and educational standards. The other reason is that you, as a director or coach, need comprehensive liability insurance, in the event that a student is hurt while participating in one of your activities and/or to protect you from lawsuits. Both of these organizations provide that insurance along with many other benefits.

> National Education Association (NEA)
> 1201 Sixteenth Street, Northwest
> Washington, DC 20036
> www.nea.org/

> American Federation of Teachers (AFT)
> 555 New Jersey Avenue, Northwest
> Washington, DC 20001
> www.aft.org/

—speech and drama

American Alliance for Theatre
& Education
Theatre Department
Arizona State University
P. O. Box 872002
Tempe, AZ 85287-3411
www.aate.com

Educational Theatre Association ETA
(International Thespians)
3368 Central Parkway
Cincinnati, OH 45225-2392
www.kingsandclowns.com/
School and individual memberships

National Federation Interscholastic
Speech & Debate Association
P. O. Box 690
Indianapolis, IN 46206
www.nfhs.org/
School memberships/state affiliates

www.artslynx.org/
A collection of arts organizations

Psychological & Spiritual Resources

Don't Sweat the Small Stuff... and It's All Small Stuff:
Simple Ways to Keep the Little Things from Tak-
ing over Your Life by Richard Carlson, Hyperion,
1997.

Handbook to Higher Consciousness by Ken Keyes, Jr.,
Love Line Books, 1990.

The Hero Within: Six Archetypes We Live by Carol S.
Pearson, HarperSanFrancisco, 1998.

How Can I Help? by Ram Dass and Paul Gorman, Alfred
A.Knopf: New York, 1985.
Written for the helping trades, i.e., nursing, police
work, social work, and teaching. Full of practical
insights and spiritual nurturance.

Journal of the Institute of Noetic Sciences,
475 Gate Five Road Suite 300, P. O. Box 909,
Sausalito, CA 94965
http://www.noetic.org/
Association founded by Astronaut Edgar Mitchell

to explore the frontiers of human ability...an exciting, thought-provoking favorite of mine.

Living, Loving and Learning by Leo Buscaglia, Ph.D., Fawcett Books: New York, 1990.
Words from a wise professor from the University of Southern California...a collection of his lectures.

The 7 Habits of Highly Successful People: Powerful Lessons in Personal Change by Stephen R. Covey: Fireside, 1990.

The Seven Spiritual Laws of Success: A Practical Guide to the Fulfillment of Your Dreams by Deepak Chopra: Amber-Allen Publishing, San Rafael, CA, 1994.

The Truth About Burnout: How Organizations Cause Personal Stress and What to Do About It by Christina Maslach, Jossey-Bass, 1997.

ORDER FORM (Purchase orders accepted.)

Mardel Books
6145 W. Echo Lane
Glendale, AZ 85302

Name _____

Address _____

City _____

State/Zip _____

Phone or Email _____

Price schedule: 1 book, $17.95; 2-4 books, $14.40 each; 5-99 books, $10.80 each; 100 or more, $9.00 each.

Shipping & handling add: $5 per book up to 4 books. 8% of total order for 5 books or more.

Please send me _____ **books at $** _____ **each.**

Total order: _____

AZ residents add sales tax: _____

Add applicable S/H charges: _____

Grand total: _____

UNCONDITIONAL MONEY BACK GUARANTEE: If you are not 100 percent satisfied with this text, just return your order. Your money will be refunded.